A People's History of India

Volumes published:

General Editor: IRFAN HABIB

The Aligarh Historians Society, the sponsor of the project of *A People's History of India*, is dedicated to the cause of promoting the scientific method in history and resisting communal and chauvinistic interpretations.

PEOPLE'S HISTORY OF INDIA 1

PREHISTORY

Irfan Habib

Aligarh Historians Society

 Tulika

Published by **Tulika Books**
35 A/1 (ground floor), Shahpur Jat, New Delhi 110 049

First edition (hardback) 2001; Second edition (paperback) 2002;
Third edition (paperback) 2003; Fourth edition (paperback) 2004;
Fifth edition (paperback) 2005; Sixth edition (paperback) 2006;
Seventh edition (paperback) 2007; Eighth edition (paperback) 2009;
Ninth edition (paperback) 2012

Tenth edition (paperback) 2015

ISBN: 978-93-82381-52-5

Designed by Ram Rahman and typeset in Minion and Univers
Condensed at Tulika Print Communication Services, New
Delhi, and printed at Chaman Enterprises, 1603 Pataudi
House, Daryaganj, Delhi 110 006

Contents

CONTENTS

Tables, Maps and Figures

Preface

The monograph on *Prehistory* that you hold in your hand describes the earliest ages of human life in India, long before any written records can directly or indirectly shed light on it. It is part of a larger project, A People's History of India, but is also intended to stand by itself. In Chapter 1 it treats in brief the geological formation of India, and changes in its climate and natural environment (vegetation and wildlife), in so far as these are relevant to an understanding of our prehistory and history. Chapter 2 provides the story of man, in the global context and then within India. The changes in his tool kits are related to the kinds of people who were their authors. Chapter 3 describes mainly the coming of agriculture, and the beginnings of exploitative relationships.

An effort is made in all the three chapters to draw on the latest information available in authoritative works and journals.

In this monograph as well as in the parts of the People's History that would follow, the style is sought to be kept simple, without making it 'popular', rhetorical or inexact. Use of technical terms is kept to a minimum, and an effort is made to provide a workable explanation of each term at first use. Abbreviations too are avoided, if these would not mean anything to a lay reader. Thus 'mya' or 'my' for million years ago, 'kya' or 'ky' for thousand years ago, 'AMM' for Anatomically Modern Man, or 'BP' for Before Present are not used, though these are explained for readers who may encounter these abbreviations in more technical works (see Note 2.1). A 'Bibliographical Note' is given at the end of each chapter, where the more important books and articles covering the subject of the chapter are listed with brief comments. References for quotations, if any, are also given here. Unfortunately, all printed sources used by me could not be specified in the Bibliographical Notes, which have had necessarily to be very selective.

For technical or controversial matters that need special attention, such as problems of chronology or particular theories, there are special notes, appended to the main text. Thus in Chapter 1 there is a note on Geological Ages, in Chapter 2 on Dating Methods for Prehistory, and in Chapter 3 on the Desert River (Sarasvati) controversy.

It is hoped that the chronological and other tables, maps and figures would be found to be useful aids and interesting in themselves. Where the international boundaries are shown on our maps, these conform to boundaries delineated on Survey of India maps.

It should be made clear that the use of the word 'man' or pronoun 'he', when what is intended is a reference to members of the hominid species in general, including women and men, is a concession to idiomatic usage. No particular emphasis on the masculine element should be assumed from such use.

By 'India' is meant, unless the context indicates otherwise, what it denoted before 1947, that is, the area comprising the territories of the present nations of India, Bangladesh and Pakistan. 'South Asia' further includes Sri Lanka, Afghanistan, Nepal and Bhutan. 'Indian Union' indicates always India with its post-1947 frontiers. Both Sri Lanka and Afghanistan have been freely brought into our narrative, and so would Nepal be in subsequent parts.

It is my pleasant duty, on behalf of the Aligarh Historians Society, to acknowledge the generous grant from the Madhya Pradesh State Textbook Corporation, Bhopal, which has made this endeavour possible.

In order to ensure that the text is kept free of errors of various kinds, the text of the monograph was circulated at three stages of its genesis. I am grateful to many friends for their comments, which resulted in changes of both narration and style. Professor Suraj Bhan has been kind enough to go through the text, and to him special thanks are due.

Mr Sudeep Banerji has helped us to get the project off the ground. Professor Shireen Moosvi, Secretary of our Society, has done most of the organizing. Mr Muneeruddin Khan has carefully processed the text and borne most manfully with the constant changes made.

Faiz Habib and his senior colleague, Mr Zahoor Ali Khan, have drawn all the eight maps that illustrate the text. Much effort has gone into assuring their accuracy. It should be noted too that Maps 1.4, 2.1, 2.2 and 3.1 embody a good deal of research as well.

I should like especially to thank Dr Rajendra Prasad and Ms Indira Chandrasekhar of Tulika for their ready cooperation, the former, especially, for help in all manner of ways.

December 2001   IRFAN HABIB

Note to the Third Edition
Opportunity has been taken of this edition to make certain corrections and update information.

April 2009   IRFAN HABIB

1

The Formation of India's Physical Features and Natural Environment

1.1 The Geological Formation of India

History as the story of the past is essentially a narration of change. We see changes occurring constantly around us. Over longer periods not only human beings' ways of life but also the patterns of their thought, beliefs, language and customs, have been constantly subjected to change. Charles Darwin showed nearly a hundred and fifty years ago that all species (including the human) have altered and evolved through processes that have gone on for millions of years. And it was already established before Darwin that the earth's surface itself has also changed hugely over time, though here we have often to think in terms of hundreds or even thousands of millions of years.

The formation of the earth itself is now usually dated to a time 4,600 million years ago. Radioactivity has revealed to us that the oldest rocks on the earth's surface go back to some 4,030 million years. They thus belong to the Archean age (4,000 to 2,500 million years ago) in 'Geologic time' (see Table 1.1, p. 18), during which life also arose in the form of the earliest algae and bacteria. While life developed in diverse ways, the appearance of the earth's surface or 'crust' also altered constantly. According to one theory, the earth has been growing in size (by reducing its own density) so that its present diameter is about two-thirds larger than what it originally was. This means that the area of the earth's surface has become larger and larger during the 3,500 million years that there has been life on this planet. There is evidence that land masses which are now far apart were once united: this is especially inferred from the fact that the orientations of palaeo-magnetism in their rocks (their 'pole paths') would conform to each other only if these were once closely adjacent. Such earlier attachment, based on fits of geographical forms (as between Africa and South America), had been suggested by the older theory of 'Continental Drift'. What is now India is supposed, in this theory, to have belonged to a supercontinent designated 'Gondwanaland' situated in the southern hemisphere. Gondwanaland (named after Gondwana rocks in

1

central India) is thought to have comprised India, Australia, Antarctica, Africa and South America. The fact that India once belonged to this supercontinent has been supported by the discovery of fossils (that is, traces of bodies of living things found in rocks) of closely akin species in all these areas in earlier geological times. This similarity between at least Australia and the rest tends to cease after the end of the Jurassic period (144 million years ago), when the various parts of this supercontinent are supposed to have started to pull apart. The portion later to form India moved north to join the Eurasian continent (comprising much of the present land mass of Europe and Asia) some time during the Eocene epoch (58 to 37 million years ago). (See Map 1.1.)

MAP 1.1 The world 230 million years ago

Drifts of land masses after Jurassic (144 million years ago) indicated thus: ------>
Note the long journey of India.

2

This process of the scattering of such a large land mass is now attributed partly to the expansion of the ocean-floor. Studies of undersea ridges have suggested that the sea-floor has been constantly pushing against land. This process is also linked to the formation of tectonic plates. The present understanding is that India, Australia and the Indian Ocean constitute a plate—the Indian Plate—which presses against the African Plate on the west and the Eurasian Plate on the north. These plates rest on a hypothetical lower soft layer called the 'Asthenosphere' on which each plate would slide, were it not constricted by other plates. The friction between the plates, with a 'convergent' motion on one side balanced by a 'divergent' one on another, has constantly changed land-forms by pushing up or pressing down land along the fault-lines. (See Map 1.2.)

MAP 1.2 'India' 65 million years ago, with boundaries of tectonic plates

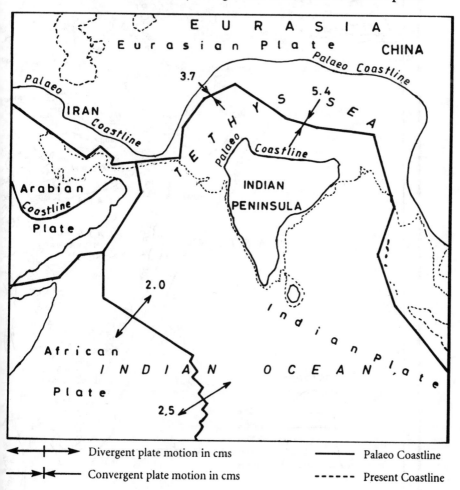

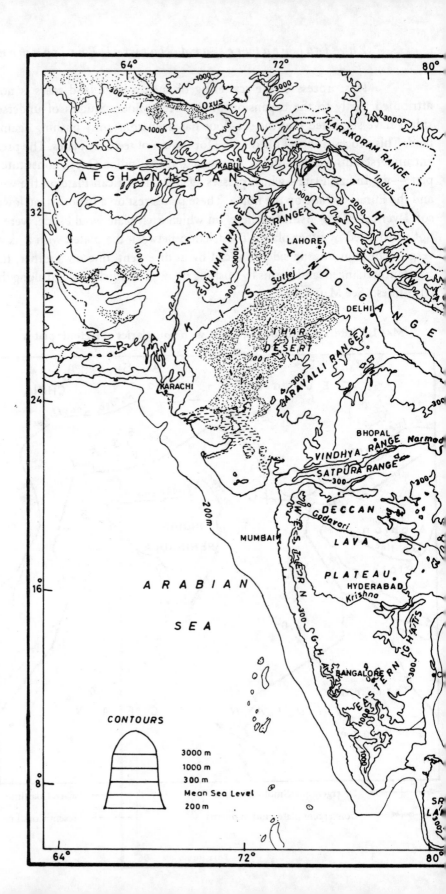

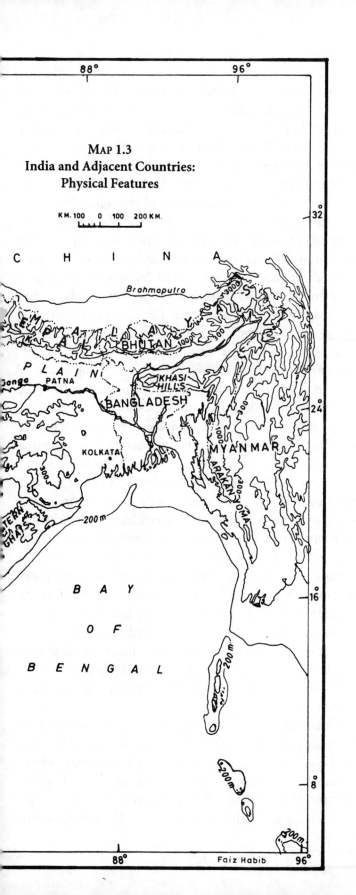

MAP 1.3
India and Adjacent Countries:
Physical Features

KM. 100   0   100   200 KM.

C   H   I   N   A

Brahmaputra

HIMALAYAS

BHUTAN

PLAIN

Ganga   PATNA

KHASI HILLS

BANGLADESH

MYANMAR

KOLKATA

ARAKAN YOMA

WESTERN GHATS

200 m

B   A   Y

O   F

B   E   N   G   A   L

200 m

200 m

200 m

Faiz Habib

88°   96°   32°   24°   16°   8°

As under these various impulses both land-forms and sea-limits have constantly altered, it would be difficult for us to establish the time when one could have recognized India by its present physical features even roughly on this globe. But by the end of Palaeozoic times (248 million years ago) the shape of the Deccan or peninsular India was at least not very different from what it is now. Its base is mainly built up of rocks formed in Archean times, which makes the Indian peninsula one of the oldest and geologically most stable blocks on earth. Indeed, stuck vertically to its northern edge, the Aravallis are thought to be one of the oldest still surviving mountain ranges of the world. The earlier Deccan rocks do not contain any fossils, but the Gondwana rocks, belonging to the Carboniferous times (320 to 286 million years ago), have fossils of land organisms. This suggests that by about 300 million years ago the Deccan was already a mass of land uncovered by sea. Before the end of the Lower Cretaceous period, or about 98 million years ago, the Gondwana rocks have fossils of dinosaurs, or the great reptiles.

In the Himalayas and the Salt Range, rocks containing fossils of marine life go back to the Cambrian period (up to 570 million years ago), which shows that these rocks have developed out of sea sediments, and that where we have the Himalayas now was once a sea. It could have been a part of what the geologists call the Tethys Sea, which is supposed to have extended from the Mediterranean to China. Marine fossils in the Himalayas are found until the end of the Mesozoic age (that is till about 65 million years ago), and western Rajasthan and Kutch have yielded marine fossils of Jurassic times, 213 to 144 million years ago, so that these too must then have been covered by sea.

Massive volcanic activity took place in the north-western parts of the Deccan and Gujarat in the Cretaceous period (144 to 65 million years ago), and the resulting lava flows and ash-beds—'the Deccan Trap'—cover an area of over half a million square kilometres. From the beginning of the Tertiary period (65 million years ago), and especially in the Eocene epoch, the Himalayas began to rise, a momentous lift that continued into Miocene (25 to 5 million years ago). It was during the Miocene epoch that the earliest apes appeared on the scene. It is believed that the Himalayas and related mountain chains arose out of the severe folding caused by the pressures of the Indian Plate against the Eurasian Plate.

From the Himalayas large amounts of broken rock and alluvium were brought down by glaciers and rivers to form the Siwalik Hills along the foot of the Himalayas, a process of secondary hill formation which continued down to perhaps one million years ago. At the same time the alluvium was continuously deposited through Himalayan drainage below the Siwaliks so that by the Pleistocene epoch (1.8 million to 10,000 years ago) the

Tethys Sea, here varying in depth from 2,000 to 6,000 metres, was filled up and the great alluvial basins of the Indus and Ganga–Brahmaputra rivers were formed.

1.2 Physical India since the Coming of Man

The earliest humans (*Homo habilis* or *Homo erectus*) appeared in the Salt Range (Pakistan) and the Siwaliks (India) about two million years ago, just before the beginning of the geological epoch of Pleistocene. Though the physical features of India were then by and large similar to those today, some processes, such as Himalayan uplifts and rock accumulations in the Siwaliks, continued during Pleistocene. Some other parts of the world were much more affected than India by repeated phases of glaciation (Ice Ages), which were a special feature of the nearly two million years of Pleistocene. During the Ice Ages large areas of northern Europe and Asia were covered by ice, and the glaciers (bodies of ice moving down slopes, channels, or valleys), became larger and longer. During such times ice-sheets covered the Himalayas down to a line running at about 1,800 metres above sea level, as against 4,000 metres today. The Himalayan glaciers then took over large upper sections of river courses that they had previously fed, coming down to as low as 1,400 metres above sea level, these points being now marked by terminal moraines, or accumulations of earth and rocks deposited by the glaciers. Glaciers have also left their mark by altering physical contours through removing rocky obstructions, digging up deep hollows and even levelling down hills.

In India, as all over the world, a major result of glaciation in each Ice Age was a great fall in sea level, since enormous bodies of water were kept frozen in large ice-sheets in north-western Europe and northern America. It is believed that in the last Ice Age in late Pleistocene, the sea level was between 100 and 150 metres below the present mean sea level. Such a retreat of the sea in the Ice Ages meant that both the Gulf of Kutch and the Gulf of Cambay became stretches of dry land; Sri Lanka was joined to south India by a broad belt of land around Adam's Bridge; and the north, middle and south Andaman Islands formed a single island. Such land bridges allowed animals, including hominids and early members of our own species, to reach areas which are now islands. However, in the numerous inter-glacials, when warmth returned, the sea rose again to reclaim all of the lost land, just as it did after the beginning of the present epoch, that of Holocene, 10,000 years ago. During some of the especially warm inter-glacial phases, the sea level could have risen even above the present sea level. A study of coral deposits shows the sea level to have been higher about 1,20,000 years ago and then 30,000 years ago. Within Holocene, which is really the present interglacial, it also possibly rose some 5,000 years ago to a level 3 metres above the present one. In such situations, the Rann of Kutch could well have become a seasonal, shallow inlet of the sea, and much of deltaic Bangladesh covered by sea.

Despite the changes in ice-sheets and sea coasts, we must remember that in Pleistocene the three major regions constituting India were fixed in the same latitudes as they are today and with roughly the same limits and altitudes. These regions are:

(1) The southern or peninsular block, which had long ago obtained its present form, with its higher edge placed in the west and the plateau sloping down eastward.

(2) The northern plains, built up of alluvium from the Himalayas. The Aravalli Range with its spurs thrown north-eastwards divides the plains into two natural parts, namely, the Indus and Gangetic basins.

(3) The Himalayas, extending the whole way in the north, with associated mountain chains running down to the sea, in the east and the west.

Still, a physical map of India at the dawn of Pleistocene (1.8 million years ago) and before the Ice Ages could have been much different from that of the present day. For one thing, there could have been great differences in the way rivers flowed in the northern plains. It was in fact once argued that, instead of the two major river systems—the Indus and the Ganga–Brahmaputra—there was one system only, that of the 'Indo-Brahm' or 'Siwalik' river, flowing from east to west along the Himalayas and then turning south to fall into the Arabian Sea. Such theories are no longer held; but this, at least, is certain, that either the Yamuna once flowed into the Indus, or the Sutlej flowed into the Yamuna. The simple reason for this is that both the Indus and the Ganga have the same species of dolphins. This could only happen if one major tributary of either had shifted from the Ganga to the Indus or vice versa, within the last million years.

The geological epoch we are today living in is known as Holocene. It began some 10,000 years ago after the last Pleistocene glaciation had ended. During this period the physical map of India (see Map 1.3) has remained quite stable, the changes occurring in physical contours (lines of height above mean sea level), coastlines and river systems having been relatively minor. If one forgets man's handiwork in running rivers dry through irrigation, or creating large inland lakes through dams and dykes, or cutting and blasting away rocks, a major factor for change on land has been earthquakes. These are, in the main, attributed to the pressure of tectonic plates striking against each other, thereby generating frictions of enormous magnitude. The Himalayas lie along such a series of fault-lines, and the tectonic movements that have pushed them up may still be at work. The Assam earthquake of the year 1897 even altered the heights and relative positions of the hills, an effect also seen in the earthquake of 1950 in the same region. In 1819 an earthquake in Kutch in Gujarat depressed a part of the Rann to let in sea water, while raising a remarkable dyke (Allah Bund), 3 to 5.5 metres high and 80 kilometres long. The recent earthquake of January 2001 in the same area has again affected ground levels in various parts of the Rann.

Much change in coastlines has also occurred during Holocene: at its beginning, 10,000 years ago (8000 BC), the sea level was probably 100 metres below the present level, but as the large ice-sheets formed during the last Ice Age melted, the sea level rose to roughly the present level by 5000 BC, whereafter the fluctuations have been on a decreasing scale. Such fluctuations are the reason why trees were found submerged in the sea up to a depth of 4 metres below the low-water mark east of Mumbai island; and there has been subsidence on the north-western tip of the Saurashtra coast, at Dwarka, where some submerged Indus culture remains have been found. The deltas of alluvium-laying rivers have been advancing into the sea, but not in any regular fashion, or along uniform fronts. Where the main river discharge occurs the land advances, but simultaneously elsewhere previously deposited alluvium is encroached upon by the sea. In the Ganga–Brahmaputra delta of Bangladesh, it is hardly possible for a map of the deltaic islands made one year to stand true the next. In the net, however, the pace of advance of the shoreline of the deltas of even the larger rivers has not been as great as some map-makers (for example, Schwartzberg) have tended to assume. The Indus culture sites of Tharro and Koonj Sor, for example, rule out any advance of more than 40 or 60 kilometres in 4,000 years for the shoreline along the Indus mouths; indeed, the actual advance in the net might have been far less.

As for the rivers, their courses in the mountains and hill valleys have remained fixed to within very narrow limits. In parts of the alluvial plains of north India, too, alterations of courses during Holocene have been rather limited. The Indus has a fixed course between the Salt Range on the east and the Sulaiman Range on the west. Similarly, the Ganga and Yamuna in their upper courses have excavated such deep beds for themselves below the surrounding plains, as make it seem very unlikely that within the last 10,000 years or more they could have flowed in any direction other than the one they take now. Generally speaking, rivers cannot flow against the contours or cut across existing drainage-lines, as indicated by directions of channels of smaller streams and nullahs. Still, some rivers of the Indus–Ganga plains have been known to change courses quite radically within the last millennium itself. The

Ravi used to flow east of Multan, but some time before the sixteenth century, it ran straight into the Chenab north of Multan, as it still does. The Beas after uniting with the Sutlej separated again to run well north of it, a course abandoned by it only in the seventeenth century. In Bihar the Kosi is notorious for altering its channels over a large area. In Bengal, the Tista abandoned the Ganga to flow directly into the Brahmaputra in the eighteenth century, while the Brahmaputra abandoned the great eastward curve of its main bed (still bearing its name), and now runs almost due south to join the Ganga.

In the Deccan peninsula, the rivers have generally long narrow valleys in the plateau, and so it is only near the coast that shifts of channels can occur. The Kaveri, after a stable course, divides into two branches near Tiruchirappalli; of these, the Coleroon today carries the main river, but earlier the other branch, still carrying the river's name, was probably the main bed of the river.

1.3 Climate

We have seen that when the 'Continental Drift' had ceased and the main land-forms of India had been created, some time before the onset of Pleistocene, about two million years or so ago, India was already situated within the same degrees of latitude as at the present day. Latitudes are parallel lines that divide the space lying between the Equator (or Latitude $0°$, forming the longest line of latitude) and the two Poles ($90°$ North and $90°$ South, which are just points). Since any area near the Equator gets a greater amount of the sun's rays than an area of equal size closer to either of the two Poles, countries lying between degrees of latitude of lower numbers and so closer to the Equator, are warmer than those lying among higher latitudes, closer to the North or South Pole. The mainland of India lies between Latitude $8°$ North and a little above $37°$ North, and these being 'low' latitudes, its climate is basically warm (Tropical). It was for this reason that during the Pleistocene Ice Ages, the ice-sheets and glaciers remained confined to the Himalayas, and this possibly made it easier for the early humans to enter India and make it their home.

The second factor that modifies the temperatures prevailing in any area is its altitude, or relative height, which is measured in relation to the mean sea level (that is, the heights are read as so many metres above sea level). The higher a place, the thinner the air and so the lower the temperature. The Himalayas and the associate parallel range of the Karakoram are the highest mountain ranges in the world and thus have the largest permanent ice-sheets outside the two polar regions; the climate throughout these ranges is accordingly cold (Alpine). In the southern peninsular block, too, the higher hills and elevated plateaus have a much milder climate than the lowland plains.

The great geological stresses which pushed up the Himalayas also contributed to making the rest of India much warmer. This is because the Himalayas bar the southward path of winds blowing from the colder regions of the north. Comparisons with areas in the American plains of the same latitudes as the Indo-Gangetic plains have shown that the Himalayan barrier has made the Indian plains warmer by 1.5 to 3 degrees Celsius.

The fact that the southern peninsula has large oceanic expanse on both sides, the Arabian Sea on the west and the Bay of Bengal on the east, helps greatly to moderate the climate of the Deccan. Compared to land, the sea heats and cools far more slowly, so that its proximity prevents land temperatures from rising or falling as much as they would at places further inland. Moreover, when the land mass heats up the air over it rises, and cooler winds blow in from the sea to cool the lower atmosphere. The peninsula thus never experiences the extremes of temperatures that occur in northern India.

The other important element of climate, besides temperature, is rainfall—or rather, 'precipitation', which comprises all deposits of water through rain, mist, snow, sleet and hail. The rainfall regime in India is mainly determined by temperatures that develop over its land mass and over the Arabian Sea and the Bay of Bengal. This is because the Himalayas, together with the mountain ranges running north–south on both the west and east of India, prevent surface wind movements across them. Thus when during summer, the plains of the north and the Deccan peninsula heat up, there is no inward wind movement from the Asian land mass, but cooler, water-laden winds—the south-eastern 'monsoon'—move in from the Arabian Sea and the Bay of Bengal. Monsoon winds from the Bay of Bengal strike the eastern hill barrier and the Himalayas to turn west and move across the plains. They weaken as they move west, and so the rainfall decreases sharply towards the northwest. It is this diminution which is responsible for the Thar Desert of Rajasthan and Sind. During winter the direction of the winds reverses as they (the 'returning monsoons') blow from the cooler land mass towards the sea. The rain they bring is of continental origin, that is, from evaporation of surface water only, and so the late-winter rains are very light. This is not true, however, with regard to coastal Andhra Pradesh, Tamil Nadu, and northern and eastern Sri Lanka, where the winter monsoons come laden with water from the Bay of Bengal. (For distribution of rainfall, see Map 1.4.)

Given the fact that the great mountain barrier had been built long before the beginning of Pleistocene, there can be little doubt that the monsoon regime as we know it today must be two million years old, at the very least. During the Ice Ages, as the sea retreated rainfall must have diminished

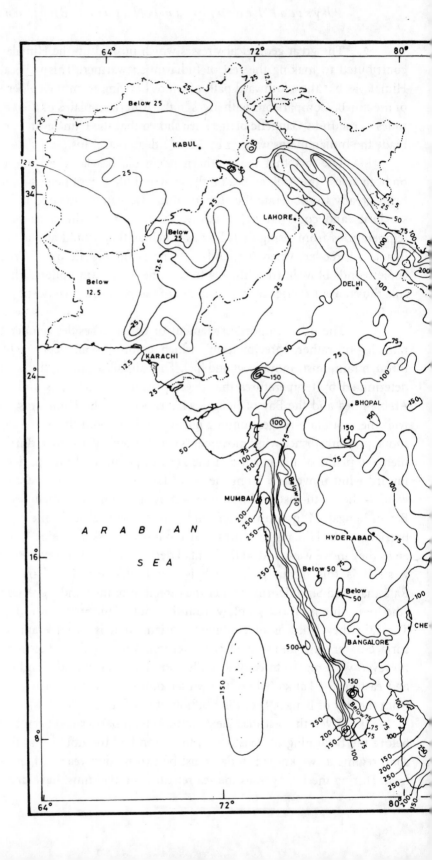

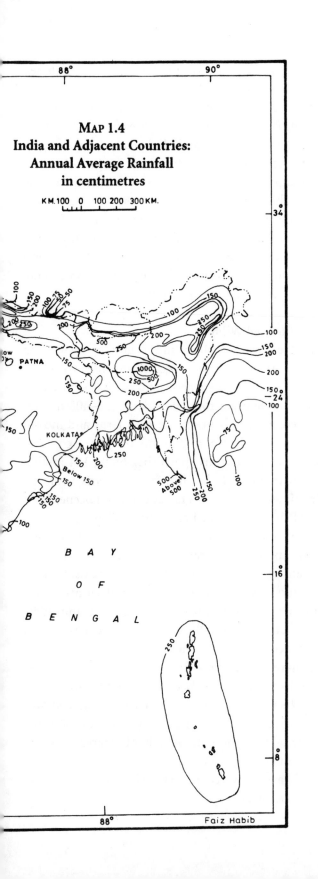

Map 1.4
India and Adjacent Countries:
Annual Average Rainfall
in centimetres

KM.100 0 100 200 300KM.

PATNA

KOLKATA

Below 150

Above
500

B A Y

O F

B E N G A L

Faiz Habib

considerably, whereas it must have increased during the inter-glacial phases, such as Holocene, during which we ourselves live.

There has been some debate about whether during Holocene there have been changes in rainfall, it being proposed from examination of the Rajasthan lake-beds that there have been 'wet' and 'dry' phases for one or two thousand years or more at a stretch. Some practitioners of 'archaeoclimatology' have also postulated a southward shift of the monsoons over the period 4000 to 2000 BC. It is also possible that rainfall has decreased during the last two or three thousand years owing to the cutting down of forests and the extension of cultivation at the expense of natural vegetation. Such change, then, has been mainly due to man's interference with nature, since the removal of permanent plant cover greatly reduces ground retention of water and, thereby, the amount of locally-originating precipitation.

1.4 Natural Vegetation and Wildlife

Life appeared in the form of algae and primitive bacteria in Archean times, some 4,000 to 2,500 million years ago. Marine life evolved by Cambrian times (beginning 570 million years ago), and earliest land plants and insects are found fossilized in Silurian rocks datable to 438–408 million years ago. But these plants were extremely primitive; even ferns and mosses appeared only in the Devonian period (408 to 360 million years ago), and flowering plants only in the Lower Cretacious epoch (beginning 144 million years ago). The lower Gondwana rocks in India yield fossils of ferns, while the upper ones have fossils of conifers. The earliest grasses came in Eocene, 55 to 38 million years ago. It is probable that by the beginning of Pleistocene, over 1.8 million years ago, the vegetation in the form of trees, bushes, shrubs and grasses was such as would have appeared familiar to us, though on closer scrutiny we would have found many species of plants that no longer exist today.

Within the two million years of Pleistocene, vegetation must have altered in character over much of the land mass as the Ice Ages and inter-glacials followed one upon the other. During the Ice Ages, as we have seen, a great area in the Himalayas was covered with ice, and in the plains and peninsular India the climate must have become very dry. In such conditions there must have occurred much desiccation. It is likely that the mobile sand-dunes which are now found only in the north-western part of Rajasthan and adjoining areas were far more extensive in the Ice Ages, coming up to the western face of the Aravallis and ranging beyond Jaipur well into Haryana, where these now form stationary mounds. In previous inter-glacials as much as in Holocene, vegetation would have recovered much land back from the desert as well as from the Himalayan ice-sheets.

What vegetation there was before man began to cut forests or clear land for cultivation and set his cattle to graze over the rest, is often called natural vegetation. Broadly speaking, the density and richness of plant cover in natural conditions, as these stood, say, at the dawn of Holocene, 10,000 years ago, should have varied in proportion to rainfall—the plant cover being denser and richer where the rainfall was heavier. In Bengal and coastal Orissa, the forest must have been 'wet evergreen'; elsewhere, where the rainfall was less, it would have been 'moist deciduous', with its trees seasonally losing their leaves once a year. It is often supposed that one can establish what the original natural vegetation was by looking at the plant cover in the 'reserved' forests and wastelands today. Such vegetation, however, is frequently the result of 'biotic degradation', that is, the alteration of natural vegetation by human action (through cutting down of trees, or burning of forests and scrub) or cattle-grazing (off grass and leaves). In other words, a large part of what appears on natural vegetation maps as the 'tropical dry deciduous forest', covering most of Uttar Pradesh and western Bihar, was earlier probably indistinguishable from the moist deciduous forest that is now shown on the maps as ringing it towards the north, east and south. We have already seen that where such natural vegetal cover existed, there must have been greater surface retention of water and so heavier rainfall. This would make the forests both more moist and denser still. Even in areas such as Baluchistan there could have been greater rain, which explains the presence there of dried-up trees near streams or embanked tanks that are now wholly dry.

It is also likely that before cultivation and grazing began to transform or destroy natural vegetation, some of what now survives as 'tropical thorn forest' with stunted scattered trees, was at least a dry deciduous forest. Such forest must have once covered most of the Indus basin and the broad dry belt immediately to the east of the Western Ghats. This probably explains why the elephant once roamed freely in the Indus basin, since its remains have been found not only at Indus culture sites, but also, before 5000 BC, at Mehrgarh in the plains below the Bolan Pass, south of Quetta.

Thus, during Holocene, when the present climate had become established, humans must have found in India a fairly dense forest, except in the Indus basin, the Thar and the middle belt of the peninsula. In these areas too the aridity was probably significantly less.

Fossils have told us much about the animals that lived in India in the various geological ages. Like other parts of the world, India too was home to dinosaurs, or the giant reptiles, which included some of the biggest land animals in the whole history of life: the dinosaurs appeared in the Triassic period, beginning 248 million years ago, and became extinct by the end of the

Cretaceous period, 65 million years ago. The Gondwana rocks in India, in particular, have yielded fossils of dinosaurs. Why the dinosaurs so thoroughly disappeared all over the world has remained a mystery, and several theories, including one of the earth being struck by an asteroid, have been propounded to explain their demise. Even before their disappearance, the earliest species of birds and mammals had appeared in Jurassic times, beginning 213 million years ago. But mammals, though ultimately producing carnivorous beasts of much ferocity, had probably little role to play in the destruction of the dinosaurs.

The species of mammals multiplied in time. This can be seen in India, where during the late Tertiary and Pleistocene, there were as many as seventeen species of elephants, all now extinct: only one species, the Indian elephant, now survives in India, and there is only one other species of elephant extant in the world—the African elephant. The hippopotamus, now found only in Africa, lived in both the Gangetic basin and the Narmada valley during Pleistocene. There were species of wild horses too that are now extinct. The largest bird of today, the ostrich, was also found in India 8,000 years or so ago.

The earlier extinction of various species were probably due mainly to climatic changes: the advancing and retreating ice-sheets of Pleistocene must have played havoc with many animal species. Large-scale volcanic and tectonic activity might also have harmed animal life in earlier geological epochs. But from the appearance of the Anatomically Modern Man, especially since the Neolithic Revolution (see Chapter 3), man himself and the animals he has domesticated have become chiefly responsible for the elimination of numerous species. The extension of cultivation and grazing lands has correspondingly reduced or destroyed the natural habitats of wild animals. Once the lion was the Indian lord of the forest; its presence in India is now sustained only by the small number kept in the Gir preserve in Saurashtra. The hunting leopard or *cheetah* is no more to be found in the wild, its ranks steadily depleted through capture (it did not breed in captivity) and shooting. The tiger, responsible for as many as 866 human deaths reported in 1903, when it was already fast diminishing in numbers, is clearly an endangered species today. The rhinoceros has been eliminated in its habitats spread all over India, to survive only in north-eastern India. The elephant's domain has also similarly shrunk to a few pockets of forests.

What humans have done is to promote domesticated animals—cattle, goat, sheep, pig, horse, poultry, dog, cat, etc.—their existence and numbers linked to our needs for animal power, products or pets. Mankind has indeed acquired an awesome control over the animal kingdom. The possible dangers from an utter degradation of nature (in respect to both plants and animals) to

humanity itself are now being increasingly realized. Preserving whatever rem
ains of nature should therefore become an important part of human endeavour

Note 1.1
Geological Ages

Geology is the science that studies the physical structure of the earth, spe
cially its crust. It began with observations of how the alluvial plains were built up b
deposits of silt and boulders, or how some rocks contained layers of different texture
Alberuni, in his great book on India (AD 1035) concluded from such observations tha
'India has once been a sea which by degrees has been filled up by the alluvium of th
streams.' Still more crucial for geology has been the more recent realization that rocl
were formed as a result of immense pressures and heat generated within the earth
crust, and that different rocks must in this way have formed at different times.

Two assumptions constitute the basis of efforts at building a relati
sequence for the formation of different layers of rocks:

(1) Generally, a lower rock layer or stratum should be earlier than an upp
one. (We will presently note exceptions to this rule.)

(2) Rocks containing similar fossils, that is, traces of similar living organism
are likely to be of the same age, while those containing fossils of mo
developed species are likely to belong to later times.

The first of these two rules would apply when the strata are laid out hor
zontally without much 'folding', as in most of peninsular India. But the sequenc
would be true only for a particular locality or region. One would not be able to corr
late it with the sequence of different rock strata elsewhere. Moreover, where seve
folding has occurred, or boulders have been shifted by actions of glaciers or river
whereby the later layers may now lie under the earlier ones, even sequence woul
become harder to establish.

Fossils help us to resolve both these problems. The Salt Range in Pakista
has rock-beds that contain fossils of the trilobites or extinct marine arthropods, ve
similar to fossils of organisms found in rocks of the earliest Cambrian period (570 t
505 million years ago) in Europe. One can see that this fossileferous stratum in the Sa
Range should belong to the Cambrian period. So, even where tectonic disturbances c
boulder transfers have made stratum sequence very complex, we can still spot th
older stratum by the fossils it contains.

The basic classification of geological ages, with 'epochs' or 'series' assigne
to longer 'periods' or 'systems', these latter assigned, in turn, to particular 'eras', a
arranged in an order of sequence, was first worked out for Europe. In India, rocks an
other strata began to be similarly identified with 'systems', bearing such names a
'Dharwar', 'Cuddapah' and 'Vindhyan'. These were then arranged in an order o
sequence. The 'eras' to which the 'systems' were assigned were given rather fancifu
names, viz. 'Vedic' (the oldest, and so identical with Archean of international nomen
clature), 'Purana', 'Dravidian' and 'Aryan', in that order of sequence, the last ending
with the beginning of Pleistocene. But the convenience of relating all geologica

17

TABLE 1.1 Geological Ages

Eon	Era	Period/System (Epoch/Series)	Beginning of Age (million years ago)	Organic Life
Archean			4,000	Earliest algae, and bacteria
Proterozoic	Pre-Cambrian		2,500	Colonial algae; soft-bodied invertebrates
Phanerozoic	Palaeozoic	Cambrian	570	Fish
		Ordovician	505	Corals
		Silurian	438	Land plants and insects
		Devonian	408	Ferns, mosses; amphibians
		Carboniferous		
		Lower	360	Winged insects
		Upper	320	Reptiles
		Permian	286	
	Mesozoic	Triassic	248	Dinosaurs
		Jurassic	213	Birds, mammals
		Cretaceous		
		Lower	144	Flowering plants, Dinosaurs ascendant
		Upper	98	Last age of dinosaurs
	Cenozoic	Tertiary		Dinosaurs extinct
		Paleocene	65	Large mammals
		Eocene	55	Grasses
		Oligocene	38	
		Miocene	25	Apes
		Pliocene	5	Hominids
		Quarternary		
		Pleistocene	1.8	Human species; cattle, elephant, horse
		Holocene	0.01	–

formations to a single international classification is so great that the original European scheme with continuous modifications and improvements has now been adopted everywhere, including India.

In this scheme (see Table 1.1), classification is mainly based on organic or biological forms traceable through the fossils found in the rocks, though other factors have also been considered. Pleistocene, the last but one 'epoch', is marked by the appearance of species of humans (*homo*), horses (*equus*), cattle (*bos*) and elephants (*elephas*). Studies of changes in the magnetic poles have suggested that there was a change to normalcy in magnetic polarity around 1.9 or 1.8 million years ago (the so-called 'Olduvai event'), and though this has little to do with the animal species that had by now evolved, this date is often regarded as marking the beginning of Pleistocene.

Advances in the physical sciences have made it possible to date geological changes in absolute terms with a reasonable degree of approximation. A major breakthrough was made with the 'potassium-argon (K-Ar)' method, by which rocks can be dated from 100,000 up to 3,000 million years ago. Similarly, the study of 'palaeo-magnetism' enables a rock to be dated through the determination of its magnetic phase. (For both these methods, see Note 2.1 in Chapter 2.) As a consequence, the geological ages shown in Table 1.1 can now carry dates that have a certain degree of reliability.

Many other matters are, however, far from settled. The standard division of Pleistocene based on four or five major glaciations or Ice Ages and the intervals or inter-glacials between them, has now been abandoned, the glaciation phases having been found to be much more numerous and of greatly varying intensity. The factors that caused them are also a subject of debate. There is renewed interest now in an ear-lier suggestion that the glaciations have been brought about by variations in solar energy received by the earth, the variations being caused by minute cyclical changes in the earth's orbit and precession on its axis. However, other factors, such as the effects of the Continental Drift on oceanic currents, are also being urged.

Note 1.2
Bibliographical Note

The *Imperial Gazetteer of India*, new edition, Vol. I, issued in 1907, contained chapters on geography, geology, climate, flora and fauna, written by recognized experts at the time. *The Gazetteer of India: Indian Union*, Vol. I, 'Country and People', issued by the Government of India in 1965, covers the same themes with contributions from experts of similar stature. Both publications are by now naturally dated, but still provide much basic information.

S.M. Mathur, *Physical Geology of India*, National Book Trust, 1986 (reprint 1991), updates the information on geology. The quotation from Alberuni in Note 1.1 is from Edward C. Sachau, *Alberuni's India*, London, Vol. I, 1910, p. 198.

For geography in all its aspects, the classic work still is O.H.K. Spate and A.T.A. Learmonth, *India and Pakistan: A General and Regional Geography*, Methuen, London, 1967. This covers not only India within its pre-1947 frontiers (Bangladesh then not having been separated from Pakistan), but also has a chapter on Sri Lanka by B.H. Farmer, and contains short geographical accounts of Nepal and Bhutan.

For the physical features and political boundaries of India, Bartholomew's map of the Indian subcontinent, drawn on the scale of 1:4 million, printed in John Bartholomew & Son's *World Travel Series* (now apparently no longer available), and reproduced in parts in the moderately priced *Oxford School Atlas of India*, is excep-tionally useful. Those interested in more detailed mapping may use the Survey of India's 1:1 million-scale maps of India covering India in blocks of four degrees of latitude and eight of longitude: these are relatively inexpensive. It is unfortunate that S.P. Chatterji's ambitiously planned *National Atlas of India* was not allowed to be published in a complete form owing to official restrictions, and its individual sheets are now not easily available.

Those interested in historical geography will find the most detailed historical mapping yet undertaken in Joseph E. Schwartzberg (ed.), *A Historical Atlas of South Asia*, Chicago and London, 1978. This is good for political and dynastic history; economic and cultural mapping is less successful.

Our Table 1.1 on geological ages draws (with modifications) on the chart in *The Times Atlas of the World*, comprehensive edition, 1997, p. 12, and the table on geologic time in the *Merriam-Webster Collegiate Dictionary*, 10th edn, 1996, p. 487, to whose publishers thanks are accordingly due.

Map 1.1 is drawn partly after the map in *National Geographic*, Vol. 198, No. 2, Aug. 2000, p. 50; and Map 1.2, similarly, after the map (Tectonic Plates) in *Times Atlas of the World*, p. 13. Map 1.3 is based on Schwartzberg's Plate I.B.1. Map 1.4 has been especially compiled by Faiz Habib from Gilbert T. Walker, *Monthly and Annual Normals of Rainfall and of Rainy-days from Records up to 1920*, Calcutta, 1924. Rainfall-reporting stations were by then sufficiently numerous, and the area covered included Burma (Myanmar) as well. Other sources have been used for Sri Lanka, Nepal, Afghanistan and the eastern fringe of Iran.

2
Our Early Ancestors

2.1 The Evolution of the Human Species

The popular beliefs in creation have implied that the human species was created all at once, either through an original pair—Adam and Eve—or through other similar means. This belief was shaken when in 1859 Charles Darwin published his theory of evolution in his book *Origin of the Species*. Four years later Thomas Huxley pronounced that on the same principles, the human species too came into being as a result of a long process of evolution. The search now started for the 'missing links', that is, the intermediate species through which the Anatomically Modern Man (*Homo sapiens sapiens*) evolved from far older ape-like creatures. The evidence came mainly from 'fossils', which are traces left by organic matter whose original form or shape is now preserved in rock. When we are dealing with very long ages past, nothing of the organic material itself can be expected to survive.

The discovery was made in India, about a hundred years ago, in the Siwalik Hills, of a fossil ape termed *Ramapithecus*, found among earlier Miocene sediments (25 to 16 million years ago). It was once wrongly believed to represent an intermediate species in the evolution of mankind. It has now been found that *Ramapithecus* was probably the female of *Sivapithecus*, fossil skeletons of both having been found in Pakistan, as well as other countries. The species is related to the ape orangutan, found wild in Indonesia. It thus belonged to a branch that had taken off from the main line of hominid evolution, and we cannot count it among our ancestors. Our ancestral line, it now seems certain, actually evolved within Africa, where the two African great apes, the chimpanzee and the gorilla, evolved from species branching off from it. In Chad in Central Africa, at TM 266 has been found a skull midway between that of a chimpanzee and hominid, the species being given the name *Sahelanthropus* and dated 7 to 6 million years ago.

The crucial discovery, made in East Africa, which supplied the chief 'missing link', was that of a group of species called *Australopithecines*, dating

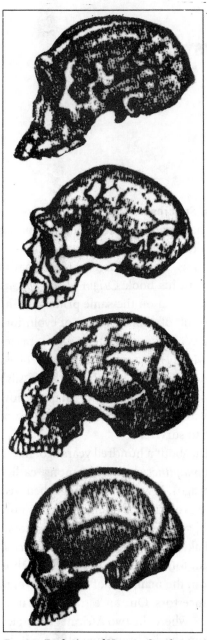

FIG. 2.1 **Evolution of Human Species: Reconstructed Fossil Skulls.** From top to bottom: *Homo habilis; Homo erectus; Homo sapiens neanderthalensis;* and *Homo sapiens sapiens* (our species).
All skulls roughly on the same scale.
(After Ian Tattersall)

back to some 4.1 million years. These, being bipeds, were true hominids. The fossil skeleton of a female—named 'Lucy' by the finders—of 3.2 million years ago, found in Ethiopia, was of a short-statured body with a cranial (brain-case) capacity of only 400 cc (compared to modern humans' cranial capacity of 1,250–1,450 cc), and belonged to a species termed *Australopithecus afarensis.* There were other similar species, of a more 'robust' (that is, heavier, thick-boned) type, all found in East and South Africa. There also developed in South Africa a rather 'gracile' (that is, thinner-boned) species called *Australopithecus africanus* with a slightly larger cranial capacity (500 cc), and going back to at least 2.3 million years ago. They could probably push or scratch with a stick, or throw a stone, but no deliberately-made tools are associated with their finds.

Species that are 'gracile' have less muscle power but can better manipulate their limbs, especially hands and fingers. Thus, *Australopithecus africanus* comes anatomically very close to what is probably the first true human species, namely, *Homo habilis* (Fig. 2.1). Found in both East and South Africa from 2.6 to 1.7 million years ago, *Homo habilis* had a cranial capacity of 700 cc and so, presumably, greater intelligence than any preceding hominid. He could make stone tools by striking one stone against another and so breaking flakes of pebbles to obtain cutting edges in the cores (see Fig. 2.2). These tools, first associated with the site of Olduvai in

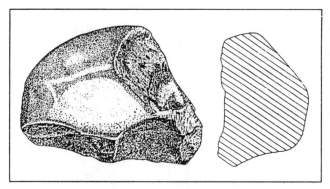

FIG. 2.2 'Oldowan' Stone Tool, *c.* **2 million years ago, from Riwat, Soan Basin.** (From *Pakistan Archaeology*, No. 24)

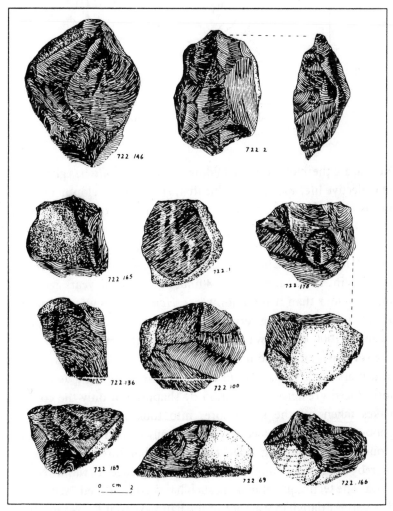

FIG. 2.3 Pebble Flake Tools from Pabbi Hills. Note: No. 722.1 (*second row from the top, centre*) is a pebble from which a large flake has been detached for use as tool. (After Syed M. Ashfaque)

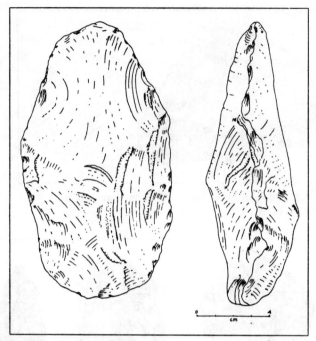

FIG. 2.4 Hand axe ('Acheulean') from Soan Basin.
(After M. Salim)

Kenya, are therefore termed 'Oldowan'. *Homo habilis* has given some evidence of collective life, and it is possible that, given the development of 'Broca's area' in his brain, he already used a series of sounds to stand for what we would today call 'words'.

    Homo habilis had a younger contemporary in *Homo erectus*, also called *Homo ergaster* in Africa (see Fig. 2.1). The dates of his anatomical fossil remains in Africa range from 1.8 million to 200,000 years ago, but the species may be older than two million years. *Homo erectus* was far more robust than *Homo habilis* and had a very heavy skull, though the cranial capacity increased to about 1000 cc. His was the first species that knew how to use and control fire (evidence of this comes from Chesowanja in Kenya, Africa, over 1.4 million years ago). *Homo erectus* first used the same tools as *Homo habilis*, but introduced greater sophistication by shaping not only the cores but also the flakes taken off the stone cores into tools, thus giving rise to a 'flaked pebble tool' industry (see Fig. 2.3). Finally came the hand axe, in which the stone had two sloping sides, and which therefore was 'bi-facial': the stone thereby obtained a rough point or a cutting edge. It was directly held by the hand. The technique of making such hand axes is called 'Acheulean' (Fig. 2.4). The earliest dated appearance of the hand axe is at Konso in Ethiopia, Africa,

1.4 million years ago. Both the Oldowan and the Acheulean techniques are taken by archaeologists to belong to the Lower or Earlier Palaeolithic (*Palaeo* = old, *lithic* = stone; so, Old Stone Age). (The term 'Lower' is used here and in other archaeological contexts for 'Earlier', because the underlying stratum is always earlier than the overlying one. Conversely, 'Upper' means 'Later'.)

2.2 Early Man in India

It was a mark of the success of the hominid species that *Homo habilis* (or an archaic *Homo erectus*) could break out of the environment of grassland and sparse forest in which he had evolved in Africa and move into areas with very different climates, extending from China (at Longgupo: a fossil jaw and Oldowan artefacts have been found which date back to 1.8 or 1.9 million years) to Spain (at Barranco Leon, 1.8 million years ago). Of similar dates are fossils of species identified as *Homo erectus* at Dmanisi (Georgia, Caucasus), 1.7 million years ago, and Mojokerto (Java, Indonesia), 1.8 million years ago. (At Dmanisi, the fossils associated with Oldowan tools are now thought by some to be of *Homo habilis.*)

Pakistan too bears traces of these earliest tools used by what was either *Homo habilis* or early *Homo erectus*. These have been found at Riwat in the Soan valley of the Potwar plateau in western Punjab, Pakistan (Fig. 2.2) and go back to about 2 million years. Similar artefacts have also been located in the Siwalik rocks in Himachal Pradesh and assigned to a similarly early date, (1.8 million years ago or earlier).

Homo habilis was supplanted in time by *Homo erectus*, whose remains in the Old World are fairly extensive. Besides his earlier traces, already mentioned, he penetrated the colder region of northern China (Zhoukuodian, 0.7 million years ago), while he continued to inhabit the densely forested island of Java (same age). His strong 'robust' physique, greater control over speech and larger brain gave him a great advantage, even when his tool-kit was still mainly based on roughly fractured pebble cores and flakes. He could use fire, to obtain warmth, scare away wild animals or make clearings, but not yet, perhaps, roast meat and bone.

In Pakistan the main flaked pebble, also called 'chopper chopping' tools in the Pabbi Hills, near Soan valley across the Jhelum, have been dated to over one million years ago (see Fig. 2.3). Similar artefacts without datable strata have been found in the Beas, Banganga and other river valleys of Himachal Pradesh. No fossils of *Homo erectus* of this age have been discovered in the entire region, but it seems almost certain that these tools were the work of this species.

The hand axe marking Acheulean industry (already known in

Africa, 1.4 million years ago) appears in the Soan valley in association with chopper chopping tools, around 700,000 to 500,000 years ago (see Fig. 2.4). Similar tools, including hand axes, are reported from Pahlgam in Kashmir on a terrace datable to a similarly early time. It is possible that armed with the hand axe which could be thrown to good effect, and with control over fire already secured, *Homo erectus* could become a hunter of smaller animals in addition to being a scavenger (eating flesh of animals killed by other predators) and a gatherer of wild fruits, roots and wild grass seeds, which he had been till then.

The spread of *Homo erectus* into the remaining parts of India took time, largely proceeding within the period the geologists call Middle Pleistocene (730,000 to 130,000 years ago). It is not possible to say how the cold dry phases corresponding to the Ice Ages which denuded the forests, and the warm moist phases of the inter-glacials which made the forests denser, impeded or aided his advance. (For these phases of the Pleistocene epoch see Chapter 1.2.) Many sites in south India including Hunsgi valley in Karnataka, and Attirampakkam, near Chennai, have turned up 'Early Acheulean tools' (of the so-

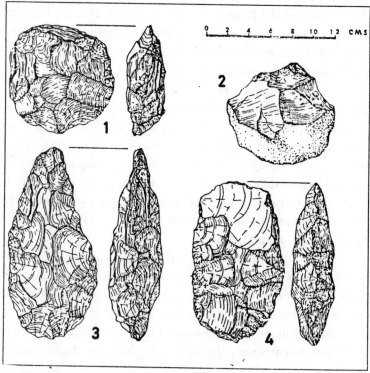

FIG. 2.5 'Madras industry' tools. (1) Discoidal core with flakes removed. (2) Chopper. (3) Hand axe. (4) Cleaver. (After B. and R. Allchin)

called 'Madras industry'), that is, hand axes, etc., made mainly from the cores (see Fig. 2.5). The U-Th method has yielded dates going back to beyond 350,000 years for sites in Karnataka. Lower Palaeolithic artefacts at Didwana in Rajasthan have been dated by the same means to 390,000 years ago, and at Nevasa in Ahmadnagar district of Maharashtra to 350,000 years ago.

During this process of his diffusion there was a tendency over time for the original *Homo erectus* to evolve into sub-species that were less robust but more dexterous, and so could make smaller tools out of flakes or the 'Late Acheulean tools'. Remains of such tools have been found in the Narmada valley, where these appear in association with the 'Narmada skull' discovered at Hathnora. This skull, belonging to an evolved *Homo erectus* could date back to a time earlier than 130,000 years ago; so too could a baby's skull, apparently of similar species, found at Odai, Tamilnadu, near Pondicherry. At the famous caves of Bhimbetka near Hathnora, successive periods of occupation begin with the lowest floors containing Late Acheulean tools.

As *Homo erectus* evolved, he also improved his tools, giving them new shapes and adjusting the technique to locally available materials. Such changes occurred very slowly, over tens of thousands of years, but these ultimately led to the rise of regional 'cultures'. The term 'culture' is used when archaeologists find at one or more sites a distinct assemblage of tools, ornaments and other products of human labour, which they call 'artefacts', as well as indications of similar customs and beliefs, such as systems of disposing of the dead, and ritual symbols. Regarding *Homo erectus*, there is little known of custom or belief, and the forms of his stone tools alone supply us with clues to his varied cultures. As the millennia passed, the tendency was for the production of smaller and thinner tools; and the apparently independent appearances of the flake blade in many parts of the world were a natural result of such a tendency. The flake blade is supposed to mark the Middle Palaeolithic stage in India. Such stone blades are found in the 'Nevasa culture' (named after the site of Nevasa already mentioned), which seems to have extended over the southern peninsula and central India (see Fig. 2.6). At Didwana, the Middle Palaeolithic is dated by the TL method to about 150,000 years, ago, but in Gujarat a date as late as 56,800 years ago has been obtained by the U-Th method. In Sri Lanka's southern wet zone, a range of 200,000 to 40,000 years ago has been suggested for it. So the culture may have lasted for a hundred thousand years, if not more. This culture is held to be in direct continuity with the Lower Palaeolithic; and, therefore, its authors were probably the direct descendants of the late *Homo erectus*, though no skeletal remains have yet been found at any of the sites.

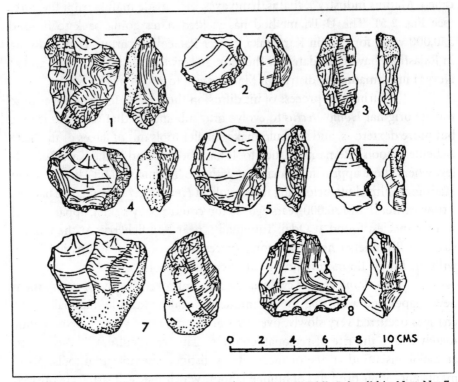

FIG. 2.6 'Nevasan' tools. No. 3 is a flaked blade, a marker of Middle Palaeolithic. Note No. 7, which shows continuance of pebble flake industry. (After B. and R. Allchin)

TABLE 2.1 Stone Age Phase, Tool-types, Species

Period	Tool-type	Species identified as first user
Lower Palaeolithic	Oldowan	*Homo habilis*
Lower Palaeolithic	Pebble flake	*Homo erectus*
Lower Palaeolithic	Acheulean	*Homo erectus*
Middle Palaeolithic	Flake blade	*Homo erectus* evolved; *Homo sapiens* archaic
Middle Palaeolithic	Levallois	Neanderthal
Upper Palaeolithic	Backed blade	*Homo sapiens sapiens*
Mesolithic	Microliths	*Homo sapiens sapiens*
Neolithic	Ground tools	*Homo sapiens sapiens*

Note: Earlier types of tools could continue to be used with subsequent tool-kits and by different species.

2.3 The Anatomically Modern Man

No presumption of such continuity with earlier cultures can, however, be made in respect of the Middle Palaeolithic tools (including flake blades) found in abundance in the Soan valley (Potwar plateau) and Rohri Hills (northern Sind) in Pakistan. In the Potwar plateau a period in the range of 60,000 to 20,000 years ago has been obtained for this 'culture' by the Carbon-14 method. There are no links at all with the Lower Palaeolithic Soan culture of 500,000 years earlier. The later industry can, then, very well be the work of the Anatomically modern (*Homo sapiens sapiens*) moving into India. It is, therefore, necessary now to turn to his origins.

Since *Homo erectus* came to be distributed over various distant regions of the Old World, each group tended to get isolated from all others, with very little gene-flow between the groups. It was inevitable that *Homo erectus* should begin to diverge into sub-species which are often classed as 'archaic *Homo sapiens*'. The tendency towards lighter bodies, or 'gracility', was widespread but by no means universal. A fairly successful robust species, *Homo sapiens neanderthalensis* or the Neanderthal Man (see Fig. 2.1), evolved in Europe out of *Homo erectus* and flourished within the period 230,000 to 30,000 years ago. There appear to have been Neanderthal settlements, from before 50,000 years ago, in West Asia and further eastward. The Neanderthaler had a short body, very narrow forehead, protruding brow-ridges, no chin, and a brain-case of about 1,450 cc, which was as large as that of the average modern human. He worked a fairly sophisticated technique of tool-making, called 'Levallois Mousterian', by which the core was trimmed first in such a manner that flakes of desired shapes could be detached. Despite all this, he had evolved in a direction opposite to that of the modern human.

The Anatomically Modern Man, or AMM, is marked, in comparison with the other hominid species, by a large forehead, the elimination of the heavy ridge above the eyes, a vertical line of the face (rather than one sloping down outwards) and a chin (see Fig. 2.1). His bones tend to be thinner, that is, he is 'gracile' rather than 'robust'. There are good reasons for supposing that our species originated in Africa and from there spread throughout the globe. The genetic diversity among sub-Saharan African peoples is the greatest compared to other human populations, and this suggests that they have undergone a much longer period of existence as *Homo sapiens sapiens* for their genes to undergo so much greater mutation than other groups of human populations. Archaeological finds have established that in Africa the modification of *Homo erectus* took place in stages. Some modern human traits are present in the *Homo erectus* found at Afar in Ethiopia (1.4 million to 600,000 years ago); then around, 200,000 years ago, an archiac *Homo sapiens* appears at

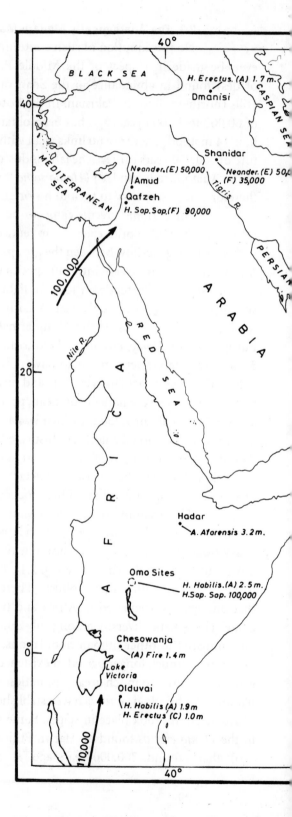

ABBREVIATIONS

Species

H. Habilis	Homo habilis
H. Erectus	Homo erectus
Neander.	Homo sapiens neanderthalensis
H. Sap. Sap.	Homo sapiens sapiens (Anatomically Modern Man)

Note: **Species** are only specified when established by fossil skeletal remains at the site.

REFERENCES

Classes of Tool Assemblages

(A) Oldowan
(B) Pebble flakes
(C) Acheulean
(D) Flake blades
(E) Levallois
(F) Backed blades
(G) Microliths

Arrows show probable lines of H. sap. sap. migrations.

Figures give number of years ago.

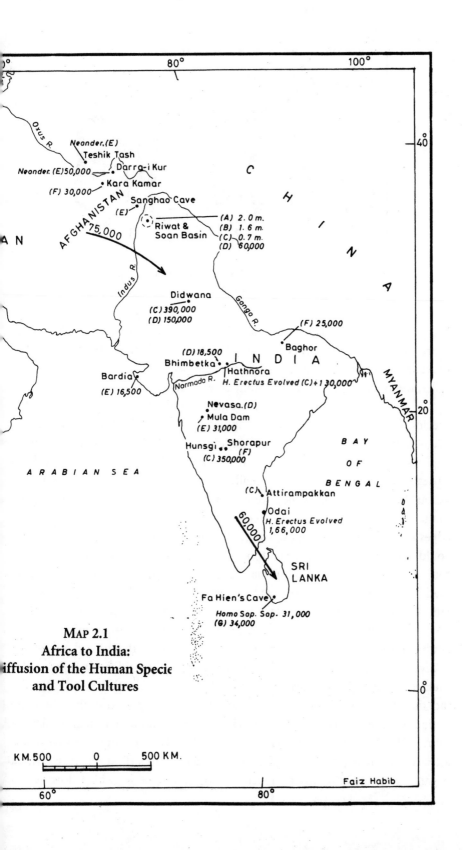

MAP 2.1
Africa to India:
Diffusion of the Human Species
and Tool Cultures

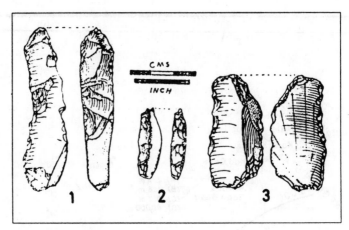

Fig. 2.7 **Backed blades from Shorapur Doab (Karnataka).**
Note small size of No. 2. (After K. Paddayya)

Elandsfontein in South Africa, in association with late Acheulean artefacts. A more evolved form appears by 120,000 years ago, sufficiently dexterous to make and handle the smaller stone tools, especially flake blades of what is called the African MSA (Middle Stone Age) industry.

Geneticists' speculations would place the original formation of the species (with an inter-breeding population of 10,000 and more) nearly 200,000 years ago. But the true Anatomically Modern Man first actually appears about 115,000 years ago in the archaeological record of southern Africa. Modern humans were initially associated with MSA tools, but then (about 90,000 years ago) they were found making thin, double-edged prismatic flakes or 'backed blades' (see Fig. 2.7). The backed blade with parallel edges seems, indeed, to be exclusively the modern man's tool, and with it he could now make diverse stone tools for different functions, and also make tools and ornaments out of animal bones and horns. The modern man also readily incorporated or took to any earlier technology, like Levallois Mousterian, or Acheulean, or pebble-flake tools, that he encountered.

With a better capacity for exhalation, he was anatomically better equipped to speak than *Homo erectus*, and it is probable that he had now greatly diversified speech. The vocal sounds were probably still frequently supplemented by gestures, whistles, intakes of breath, grunts, or other sounds. Yet the fact that despite long periods of isolation, most notably in Australia where the period possibly exceeds 50,000 years, all parts of the modern human species are found fully possessed of language of one sort or another, suggests that it was already a human attainment when the modern man's diffusion from Africa began. Language gave him a capacity to communicate with his fellow beings that was of decisive advantage in transmitting skill to one another, making possible complex and pre-planned collective actions and, not the least, providing a more convenient vehicle for storing memory and arranging thought.

2.4 The Modern Human in India

Human skeletal remains (still in fossils) attest to a very rapid diffusion of the modern man from Africa; he is found in West Asia nearly 100,000 years ago, in association with the backed-blade industry. Moving across Asia, he reached Australia over 50,000 years ago and entered the New World through Siberia and Alaska, perhaps not later than 15,000 years ago. Since the Indian borderlands were midway in his line of travel from Africa, he may have reached the periphery of the Indian subcontinent by 75,000 years ago. And he must have moved across India to reach Sri Lanka within the next 25,000 years. Modern human skeletal fossils (those of a child) have been found at Fa Hien cave in Sri Lanka, dated to 31,000 years ago, though evidence for human occupation at this site goes further back to 34,000 years ago. At Batadomba lena cave in Sri Lanka also, modern human skeletal remains of 28,500 years ago have been found. We may remember (Chapter 1.2) that though around 30,000 years ago the sea had risen, yet there would have been a direct land-bridge to Sri Lanka during the fall of sea level in an earlier phase of glaciation (50,000 years and more ago).

If we set the modern humans' first arrival in the context of an emigration across Asia leading to Australia, we must acknowledge that at the time the modern humans arrived at the Indian borderlands they could not have possessed the backed-blade technology, since they did not carry it to Australia. Backed blades are not present in the Middle Palaeolithic culture of the Soan basin in Pakistan (60,000 to 20,000 years ago), of which the modern human could have been the author. The profusion of tools and debris found at particular sites of this culture, especially in the Rohri Hills, gives us the picture of a society where some communities hunted in the plains, ravines and jungle, while others specialized in making tools in 'factories' at distant sites where good, suitable stone could be quarried. One could presume, then, that a rough division of labour and a barter system had already arisen.

In South Asia, the usual sequence of backed-blade industry marking the Upper Palaeolithic, and microliths marking the Mesolithic, appears blurred, because the sequence is rarely established by clear stratification. Nor is any Upper Palaeolithic site as early as 34,000 years ago, the date for the first appearance of microliths in Sri Lanka. Yet the logical sequence of the two technologies is so clear—it is hardly possible to imagine microliths being produced without an earlier use of tool-making backed blades—that one must assume

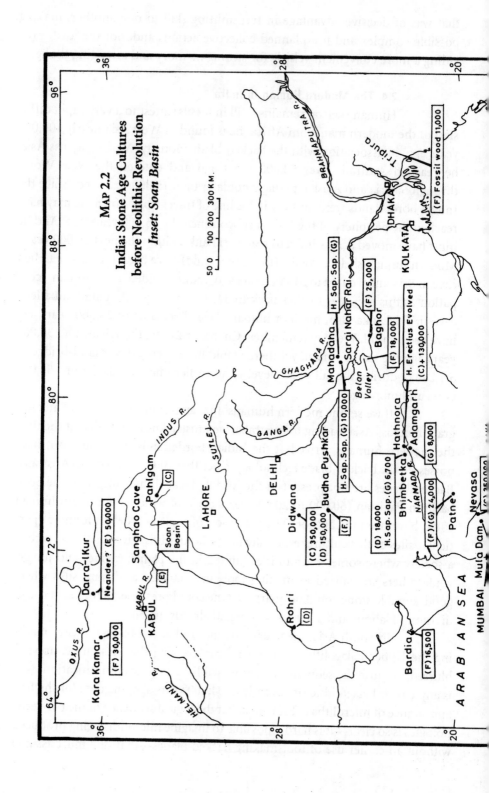

MAP 2.2
India: Stone Age Cultures
before Neolithic Revolution
Inset: Soan Basin

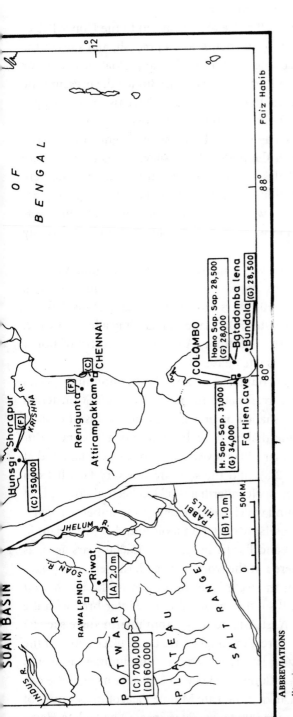

SOAN BASIN

INDUS R.

RAWALPINDI · Riwat [A] 2.0 m
SOAN R.
JHELUM R.
POTWAR PLATEAU
SALT RANGE
PABBI HILLS
[B] 1.0 m
[C] 700,000
[D] 60,000

0   50 KM

Hunsgi · Shorapur [F]
[C] 350,000
KRISHNA R.

Renigunta [F]
Attirampakkam · [C] CHENNAI

INDIAN / BAY OF BENGAL
B E N G A L
O F

COLOMBO
Homo Sap · Sap · 28,500 (G) 28,000
Batadomba lena
Bundala (G) 28,500
H. Sap · Sap · 31,000 (G) 34,000
Fa Hien Cave

80°   88°   12°

Faiz Habib

ABBREVIATIONS

Species
H. Erectus   *Homo erectus*   Neander.   *Homo sapiens neanderthalensis*
H. Sap. Sap   *Homo sapiens sapiens* (Anatomically Modern Man)

Note: **Species** are only shown when established by fossil skeletal remains at the site.

REFERENCES

Classes of Tool Assemblages

(A) Oldowan   (B) Pebble flakes   (C) Acheulean
(D) Flake blades   (E) Levallois   (F) Backed blades   (G) Microliths

Arrows show probable lines of *H. sap.* migrations. **Figures** give numbers of years ago.

that further research will provide earlier dates for the backed-blade assemblages in India than have been obtained till now.

Such early dates may well come to be assigned to the Upper Palaeolithic site of Renigunta in Chittoor district, Andhra Pradesh, and sites in the Shorapur Doab in Karnataka (see Fig. 2.7 for the Shorapur Doab artefacts), or to the backed blades from Budha Pushkar, Rajasthan. But for the present little can be said about their actual ages. In central India we have two major Upper Palaeolithic cultures, dated to about 25,500 to 10,500 years ago at Baghor I, and about 18,000 to 16,000 years ago in the Belan valley. Baghor I is a particularly significant site: located in the middle Son valley, it was a spot where stone tools, including backed blades, scalene triangles, drills and scrapers, were made in large numbers. Superstition (a very human quality!) too reigned here, since a sandstone rubble platform was unearthed, at the centre of which was a piece of ferruginous sandstone with shades of colours, which apparently represented some deity.

It is possible that there was a migration of modern human communities into eastern India from the side of Myanmar (Burma) as well. Belonging to a period 11,000 to 4,500 years ago, artefacts made of fossil-wood have been found in Tripura and eastern Bangladesh, including a backed knife. These connect with the so-called Palaeolithic 'Anyathian' industry of upper Irawaddy valley in Myanmar, in its late phase.

Did the new species encounter members of other hominid species on its arrival in India? This is a reasonable inference. Levallois Mousterian tools (made from cores initially shaped or prepared to yield tools of desired shapes) associated with Neanderthalers have been found at Darra-i Kur (50,000 years ago) and Kara Kamar (30,000 years ago) in Afghanistan, and at Sanghao cave in Pakistan (Fig. 2.8), and the sites are not very far off from Teshik Tash in Uzbekistan, where a Neanderthal skull has been discovered. At Darra-i Kur, a skull has been found which *could* belong to a member of a 'partly' Neanderthal population. If similar Mousterian tools found at Mula dam in Maharashtra (31,000 years ago) and Bardia in Gujarat (15,000 years ago), as well as other places in India, were not the work of Neanderthalers, it is possible that modern humans learnt the technique from them in the north-west and then brought it into India. If so, they might also have inter-bred with the Neanderthalers, as they did in West Asia, to judge from intermediate skeletal forms found there. Similar inter-breeding might have taken place between the modern human and the surviving late *Homo erectus* communities, as, again, happened at Ngandang in Java, Indonesia, 53,000 to 27,000 years ago. We can imagine this happening in Sri Lanka if the Late Middle Palaeolithic culture of coastal north-western Sri Lanka (74,000 to 28,000 years ago) had a late *Homo*

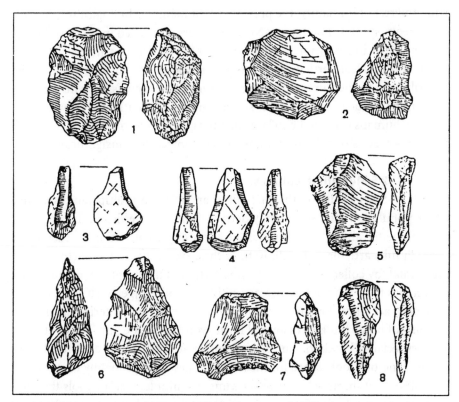

Fɪɢ. 2.8 **Artefacts from Sanghao Cave, Pakistan.** No. 1 is a 'Levallois'-prepared core from which flakes have not yet been struck off; No. 2 is a core from which the flakes have been struck off. The remainder are tools made out of the flakes. (After B. and R. Allchin)

erectus as its author, while, as we know from skeletal remains, the microlith-working human of south Sri Lanka, from 34,000 years ago onwards, was impeccably modern. (But, then, if the modern human had arrived in Sri Lanka about 60,000 years ago, he could have been the author of the other culture as well.) One must also allow that much slaughter of the rival species took place, the superior (ours!) killing the other less able to resist. The Anatomically Modern Man, thus, by both absorption and elimination, brought about the total extinction of the earlier hominid species not only in India but throughout the Old World.

Why, if inter-breeding occurred between our and other human species, the earlier species have not left some visible traits among us, is a question that has provoked much debate. It is believed that some minor physical traits of the local *Homo erectus* survive in the present-day Mongoloids of East Asia and the Australoids of Australia. But despite these minor 'racial' distinctions, and despite the long isolation of Australoid and Amerindian peoples from the rest of humanity, the present-day humanity is biologically a very homogeneous species. Though the Neanderthalers co-existed in Western Europe with modern humans for as many as 10,000 years, if not more, the recent extraction of Neanderthal DNA has not revealed any distinct Neanderthal contribution to the European gene pool. One must then assume that, both at the time of contact with the other species and subsequently, the population of modern humans came to be so large that the gene-flow from the other and less populous species or sub-species was soon dissipated into insignificance.

2.5 Mesolithic Cultures

Such ability on the part of our ancestors to multiply and sustain a larger population almost certainly derived from more efficient, lighter tools, and the better ability to communicate ideas and information to each other through fully articulate speech. Both of these would be of great help in hunting animals by collective enterprise. A reflection of the immense potential thus obtained is to be seen in the increase in the pace of change. Such change could have been accomplished by increasing the variety of tool material, making use not only of bone, but also of animal horn, wood and (in China and south-east Asia, especially) bamboo. But organic material of this kind does not largely survive, and our tool record for those early times consists mainly of stone. Yet we can see that improvements of the same magnitude in stone tools that previously took hundreds of thousands of years to come about, now took tens of thousands, and then mere thousands of years. We have the transformation, first, of the blade technology into 'microliths' (small stone tools and points, often 'bladelets', used presumably after being attached to wooden or bone handles; see Fig. 2.9), which took some seventy thousand years (100,000 to 30,000 years ago); but then, only a relatively short time elapsed between this event and the arrival of the Neolithic or New Stone Age tools, a matter merely of some twenty-five thousand years (over 34,000 to 9,000 years ago).

This transitional period, marked by microliths, is designated Mesolithic or Middle Stone Age. The earliest date for microliths in South Asia (and, perhaps, in the world) comes from Sri Lanka, where, at Fa Hien cave, simple microliths date back to 34,000 years ago, and at Batadomba lena, geometric microliths are dated to 28,000 years ago. Some microliths appear at Patne, near Chalisgaon in Maharashtra, with Upper Palaeolithic tools (about 24,000 years ago). Could there, then, have been a northward diffusion of microlithic techniques from Sri Lanka? For this we would have to suppose that short sea-crossings on canoes could now take place. Human communities now progressed from mobile groups seeking caves, rock shelters, mounds or other natural sites for temporary refuge, to partly settled populations living in pri-

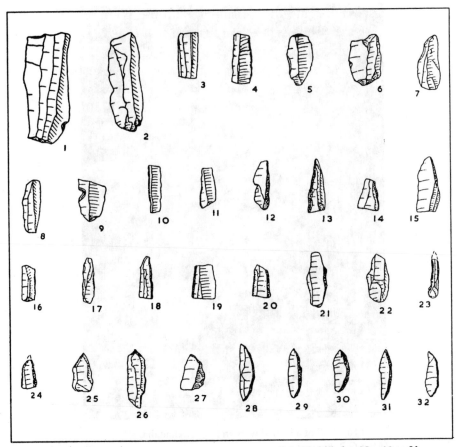

FIG. 2.9 **Microliths from Mahadaha.** Nos 1 to 9 are parallel-sided blades; Nos 10 to 21, blunted backed blades; Nos 22 to 25, points; Nos 26 and 27, burins; Nos 28 to 32, lunates. (After G.R. Sharma)

mitive huts. From the Mesolithic site of Beli lena in Sri Lanka comes evidence of charred millet grains of nearly 12,000 and 9,000 years ago (10000 and 7000 BC), suggesting that wild grains were already being collected for food. We have seen that already during the Upper Palaeolithic period, there was evidence of religious belief and symbolic representation of a deity at Baghor I. In the Mesolithic cultures such cult 'symbols' are found in ornaments, worn possibly as charms, and in scrawls on stone. The latter evolved into rock or cave art.

Among the important Late Mesolithic sites are those of Sarai Nahar Rai and Mahadaha in the same neighbourhood in the plains of central Uttar Pradesh. Sarai Nahar Rai is dated by the radiocarbon method to about 10,000 years ago (8000 BC). These sites have turned up burials with skeletons of tall (mean adult height: men, 180 cm; women, over 170 cm), large-boned, rather robust people (Fig. 2.10). The tool types had by now multiplied, but were still

FIG. 2.10 Skull of a buried woman from Mahadaha.
(After G.R. Sharma)

based on parallel-sided blades (Fig. 2.9). Arrowheads of bone and flint, with that of flint stuck into the rib of one skeleton, show that the bow and arrow had been added to the hunter's equipment. The animals hunted and eaten include *zebu* or the Indian humped ox, buffalo, sheep, goat, stag (deer), pig, rhinoceros, elephant, tortoise, turtle and different birds. There is no firm evidence that cattle or sheep or goats had been domesticated: the settlements were in forests and the animals hunted were found there in the wild state. There is evidence of fire being used to roast meat. Seeds were gathered and pounded, since stone querns and mullers have been found. Such processing suggests that the seeds might have been stored for future use. But there was no plant cultivation yet. There was no fibrous cloth to wear; probably pieces of animal skin were worn. Hair was spun into ropes by hand, but there is no evidence of weaving. There was as yet no pottery either. Ornaments of bone (pendants and necklaces) have been found at Mahadaha, apparently worn only by men, not women.

Human life was still very, very hard. The age at death of thirteen persons buried at Mahadaha has been determined, and the average falls between 19 and 28 years, being probably much closer to 19. Only one was above 40 years, and none above 50.

The burials indicate the existence of religion and superstition. Bone ornaments and bones of slaughtered animals were buried with the dead, showing a belief in after-life. Women were buried in the same manner as men; and, though there are double burials, there is nothing to show that one of the two was killed to accompany the other in after-life. A bone figurine has been recovered from the Belan valley and engraved ostrich egg shells (the bird has now long been hunted out of existence in India) from Patne in Maharashtra and Rojde in Madhya Pradesh: these were probably not made only for aesthetic purposes but had some cultic significance or superstition behind them as well.

Datable to about 8,000 years ago (6000 BC), Adamgarh in the Narmada valley represents a further advance in Mesolithic culture, with bones of domesticated animals such as dogs, *zebu* cattle, buffalo, sheep and pig appearing in equal numbers with wild animals like species of deer, porcupine and lizard. Clearly, this was a hunting community that had turned partly pastoral. Its tools were still based on parallel-sided blades, but the forms, including awls,

FIG. 2.11 'Struggle for Existence'. Bhimbetka, III C-18/a.
(Reprod. Y. Mathpal)

Above: FIG. 2.12 **Woman carrying load.** Bhimbetka,
II F-8. (Reprod. Y. Mathpal)
Below: FIG. 2.13 **Peahen.** Bhimbetka, III C-6.
(Reprod. Y. Mathpal)

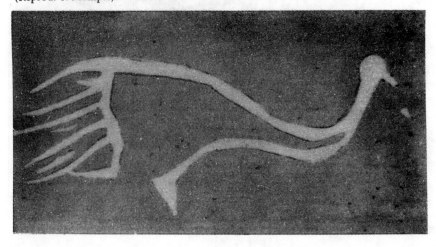

borers and burins, show considerable variety. Hand-made pottery was also found. The people lived in rock shelters, and were perhaps the first authors of cave paintings in India. The earliest paintings in Bhimbetka rock shelters near Bhopal could go back to 6000 BC (though most Carbon-14 dates are much later): they show animals being hunted by men with bow and arrow (Fig. 2.11). Human figures appear in stick-like forms. There is a striking painting of a woman carrying a load (Fig. 2.12). No inflation of particular human figures, such as might reflect a measure of distinction of rank or class within society, is discernible. Nor is there any suggestion of agricultural or even pastoral activity in these paintings. The drawing of a peahen represents genuine artistic skill (Fig. 2.13).

TABLE 2.2 Chronology of Early Humans

Years ago	
3.2 million	'Lucy', *Australopithecus afarensis*
2.6–1.7 million	Period of *Homo habilis*
2 million	Appearance of *Homo erectus* in Africa
2 million	Oldowan tools, Riwat (Pakistan)
1 million	Pebble-flake culture, Soan basin (Pakistan)
700,000 to 400,000	Acheulean culture, Pabbi Hills (Pakistan) and Himachal
500,000 to 130,000	'Narmada skull', Hathnora (*Homo erectus* evolved)
400,000 to 300,000	Lower Palaeolithic cultures of south India ('Madras industry'), Rajasthan and central India
150,000 to 50,000	Middle Palaeolithic cultures of Rajasthan, central and south India
115,000	Date of earliest fossil of *Homo sapiens sapiens* (Modern Man), South Africa
75,000 ?	Modern Man's arrival in India
60,000 ?	Modern Man's arrival in Sri Lanka
60,000–20,000	Middle Palaeolithic culture of Pakistan (Soan basin, Rohri Hills)
50,000–30,000	Neanderthalers in Afghanistan?
34,000	Appearance of microliths in Sri Lanka
31,000	Earliest fossil remains of Modern Man in South Asia (Sri Lanka)
25,500–10,500	Upper Palaeolithic cultures of Karnataka and central India
24,000	Earliest dated microliths in India (Patne, Maharashtra)
10,000	Mesolithic culture, Sarai Nahar Rai and Mahadaha (Uttar Pradesh)
8,000	Mesolithic culture, Narmada valley

Note 2.1
Dating Methods for Prehistory

In the vocabulary of archaeologists, 'Prehistory' comprises the period for which no evidence is available from written materials. When such evidence becomes available we enter the realm of 'History'. To 'Protohistory' belong cultures whose writings we are unable to read, or which are themselves non-literate but about which we can obtain some understanding or information through the evidence of their contacts with literate societies.

The cultures we have treated in Chapter 2 and are going to treat in Chapter 3 belong to Prehistory, for our entire knowledge about them comes from their physical remains only. We naturally cannot get any dates for them from any records coming down to us. Various devices are, however, available to us, especially from the physical sciences, to help us fix niches in time for particular remains or sites, and thereby for the cultures to which they belong.

First of all, when archaeological sites are excavated, strata belonging to different cultures may be found one above another. While absolute dating cannot be obtained just by the observation of strata revealed by an excavation, we can still establish sequence, for the lower strata should ordinarily belong to cultures that are earlier than those of overlying strata. Relative (not absolute) ages of different bones at the same site can be established by measuring their respective flourine, nitrogen and uranium contents. Since flourine and uranium levels in the bone increase with time, while nitrogen decreases, such measurement helps to place in sequence the cultural phases with which the different bones may be associated. Estimates of time separating one stratum from another can also be made on the basis of the thickness of the intervening deposits.

For getting absolute dates, to which relative chronology can always be keyed, a number of methods have been developed. Two such major dating techniques are based on measurements of radioactivity and magnetism.

For very early dates (from 100,000 years ago up to 3,000 million years), there is the *Potassium-Argon (K-Ar)* method based on radioactivity: the age of a piece of volcanic rock is established by measuring the proportions of potassium (K-40) and argon (A-40) contained in it.

Palaeo-magnetism is the second important method for very early dates (200 million to 780,000 years ago). Marine rocks and sediments retain the direction of the magnetic fields as it was when these were formed. The reversals of the fields took place at certain known times (established from magnetic rocks through the K-Ar method) all over the world, so volcanic rocks or sediments can be dated by determining heir magnetic phase; this date will then be true also for the fossils contained in them. Four such major reversals are known to have taken place in the last 5 million years.

These two methods are now being supplemented by others.

Rocks are being dated by *fission-tracking*. This is used for dating certain minerals embedded in the rocks through a count of fission tracks or minute tracks left by particles emitted by radioactive isotopes. The method yields dates ranging from 1,000 million to 500,000 years ago.

There are various methods of measurement of radioactive decay, such as the *Uranium-Thorium (U-Th)* method, which can give dates up to 350,000 or more years ago. The U-Th method has been used for dating certain Palaeolithic sites in India.

When dates of very early periods, as obtained from these methods, are quoted, the abbreviations 'mya' or 'my' (million years ago) and 'kya' or 'ky' (thousand years ago) are often used.

For dates of lesser ages, where greater precision is also needed, the method of determining *radiocarbon* in all organic materials has been exceptionally important. When life in organic matter becomes extinct, Carbon-14 (^{14}C), which in living matter is present in a constant proportion to Carbon-12, begins to decrease at a steady rate. This rate being known (Carbon-14 having a 'half-life' of 5,730 years), measuring the proportions of Carbon-14 and Carbon-12 in any dead organic matter would give the period of time separating the present from the moment the sample ceased to be part of a living organism. Some time after the discovery of this method in 1949, it was found that the current rate of Carbon-14 loss could not be taken to apply to the period before 800 BC, because of fluctuations in cosmic radiation. This was established particularly by matching Carbon-14 dates with *Dendrochronology*, or the chronology of climatic variations established by counting and studying annular tree-rings which tend to be thicker in wet years and thinner in dry ones. By comparing the tree-ring patterns in old, dead trees, a continuous chronology of wet and dry years has been built up for 7,000 years in California, United States. But this did not fit the one obtained by the carbon dating of the dead trees. The discrepancies could only be removed by providing for 'calibration', that is, by adding years to Carbon-14 dates, through assuming different rates for Carbon-14 loss beyond 800 BC. The calibrated dates suited much better the chronology that had been established for ancient Egypt and Iraq from documentary materials. Raw or uncalibrated Carbon-14 dates should not, therefore, be used for any period beyond 800 BC, since the differences tend to become substantial as we go further back. Thus 3000 BC obtained by carbon dating becomes 3700 BC upon calibration. Calibration based on tree-rings is now available for carbon dates up to 8000 BC, which is 9350 BC by calibration. Calibration based on coral deposits takes us to carbon date 18000 BC, which is 21650 BC by calibration. Carbon dates beyond this have to be stated just as they are, since no means yet exist of calibrating them. Dates beyond 40000 BC, if obtained by carbon dating, are not considered very reliable. But a technique, called AMS from its use of an Accelerator Mass Spectrometer, can now date very small samples of organic material, up to 100,000 years.

If carbon dates, which are always stated with standard deviations that set their probable range, are sometimes found to conflict with the established sequence of strata (a lower stratum getting a later date than an upper stratum) or to be otherwise very wayward, this may be due to a number of factors, such as the archaeologist's misreading of the stratum from which the sample came, or the contamination of the sample through attachment of later organic matter, or simple laboratory fault. In such cases, a selection of dates based on probability becomes necessary.

Carbon-14 dates are conventionally styled 'BP' or 'bp', for Before Present, the present year being taken as 1950. All 'BP' dates thus need to have 1,950 years deducted from them for conversion into BC; or, if they are lower than 1950 BP, they should be deducted from 1,950 for conversion into AD. Thus 3000 BP would be equal to 1050 BC, and 500 BP to AD 1450 . Though first employed with Carbon-14 dates, the 'BP' reckoning is now also in use with other methods.

A method useful where the object to be dated had been subjected to heat, is the one called *Thermoluminescence (TL)*. So far it has given us dates mainly of pottery. Clay, when heated, releases energy from the quartz it contains; the quartz begins to accumulate energy again once it has cooled. When this re-accumulated energy is measured, the measurement gives us the time that has passed since the clay has been baked into pottery. One can by this means date objects of up to 500,000 years in age. The method is now being extended to soils or flints subjected to fire, which can enable us to date earlier ('pre-ceramic') remains and artefacts as well.

A related method is called *Optically Simulated Luminescence (OSL)*: it is based on the fact that when a mineral is buried, the number of trapped light-sensitive electrons increases over time. When it is exposed to illumination in the laboratory, the light emitted by the electrons as they escape can be measured; and from this the time that the mineral has remained buried can be calculated.

Finally, there is a method called *Electron Spin Resonance (ESR)*, which has come more recently into use. Minerals, tooth enamel, shell and coral can be dated by this method, its range being 1 million to 1,000 years ago.

Note 2.2
Bibliographical Note

Two important summations of evidence on Prehistory, treated in a world perspective, were published in 1994. S.J. De Laet (ed.), *History of Humanity*, Vol. I: *Prehistory and the Beginnings of Civilization*, UNESCO, Paris/London, presented mainly the archaeological evidence, while L.L. Cavalli-Sforza, P. Menozzi and A. Piazza presented the genetic evidence in their *History and Geography of Human Genes*, Princeton. Both works are necessary for forming a reasoned view of what happened on the world scale. Both, however, need to be updated, as all over the world there have been new reports of archaeological finds, applications of new techniques of dating, and new genetic research. One can recommend as a well-researched textbook, Brian M. Fagan, *People of the Earth, An Introduction to World Prehistory*, 11th edn, Delhi, 2004 (a moderately priced Indian reprint). Reference to recent files of journals like *Antiquity*, London, and *Archaeology*, New York, can also keep one abreast of new data and interpretations. Ian Tattersal, 'Once We Were Not Alone', *Scientific American*, January 2000, pp. 38–44, offers an interesting discussion of our species' relationships with other extinct hominid species.

H.D. Sankalia, *Prehistory and Protohistory of India and Pakistan*, 2nd edn, Poona, 1974, is a work of detailed description, which, with many subsequent discoveries and improvements in chronology, has become partly obsolete. Bridget and Raymond Allchin, *The Rise of Civilization in India and Pakistan*, Indian edn, New Delhi, 1983, is still useful, though a little dated. Also see D.P. Agarwal, *The Archaeology of India*, London, 1982. B. and R. Allchin have updated their earlier work in a new shorter survey, *Origins of a Civilization: The Prehistory and Early Archaeology of South Asia*, New Delhi, 1997. For northern India, Pakistan and Afghanistan, chapters (including one by B. Allchin) in A.H. Dani and V.M. Masson (eds), *History of Civilizations of Central Asia*, Vol. I, UNESCO, Paris, 1992, add a Central Asian perspective. For generally updated material, see S. Settar and Ravi Korisettar (eds), *Indian Archaeology in Retrospect*, Vol. I: *Prehistory*, New Delhi, 2002, initial chapters.

For the subcontinent the volumes of *South Asian Archaeology* published at two-yearly intervals (being the proceedings of the European Association of South Asian Archaeologists) yield much rich material on Prehistory. The two major relevant Indian journals are *Man and Environment* and *Puratattva*; the quality of the latter has been rather uneven.

On researches in the Potwar/Pabbi Hills there is a good summing up in R.W. Dennell, 'The Early Stone Age of Pakistan: A Methodological Review', in *Man and Environment*, Vol. 20, No. 1, Pune, 1995, pp. 21–28. See also articles by S.M. Ashfaque and Saleem ul Haq and by B. Allchin and R.W. Dennell in *Pakistan Archaeology*, No. 23, 1987–88, pp. 1–42, and No. 24, 1989, pp. 1–20. Also see M. Salim, 'The Palaeolithic Cultures of Potwar', in *Journal of Central Asia*, Vol. 20, No. 2, Islamabad, 1997.

On the blade-tool industry of the Shorapur Doab see K. Paddayya's paper in S.B. Deo and M.K. Dhavalikar (eds), *Studies in Indian Archaeology*, Bombay, 1985, pp. 165–90. For Sarai Nahar Rai and Mahadaha, see G.R. Sharma, V.D. Misra *et al.*, *From Hunting and Food Gathering to Domestication of Plants and Animals* ... (*Excavations at Chopani Mando, Mahadaha and Mahagara*), Allahabad, 1980. The human skeletons at Mahadaha are described on pp. 86–98. On the various stone technologies, there is a useful explanatory chapter by Vidula Jayaswal in A.K. Bag (ed.), *History of Technology in India*, Vol. I, New Delhi, 1997, pp. 1–27.

Yashodhar Mathpal, *Prehistoric Rock Paintings of Bhimbetka, Central India*, New Delhi, 1984, gives accurate reproductions of the paintings at Bhimbetka, with detailed technical information.

On dating methods see D.P. Agrawal and M.G. Yadava, *Dating the Human Past*, Pune, 1993. Gregory L. Possehl's *Radiocarbon Dates for South Asian Archaeology*, University of Pennsylvania, Pennsylvania, 1989, with subsequent re-issues, is an important reference aid.

3

The Neolithic Revolution:
The Coming of Agriculture and
Domestication of Animals

3.1 Meaning of 'The Neolithic Revolution'

Man's stone tools in the earlier times were made by striking stone against stone, which left the surface rough and asymmetrical. At a very late stage these began to be supplemented by ground tools, which were made by rubbing stone against stone, or by hand-rotating softer stone on a block of stronger stone. These tools, therefore, could have smooth surfaces, and well-rounded and symmetrical shapes (Fig. 3.1). They could also be given much sharper points. Whether serving as axes with smooth long edges, or as tips of digging sticks, or as arrowheads, these were generally far more effective than the old Palaeolithic or Mesolithic tools. The famous archaeologist V. Gordon Childe (1892–1957) noted that these Neolithic or New Stone age (*neo* = new, *lithic* = stone) tools were associated with very important changes in man's material life. The ground tools themselves could have been developed out of the pounding and rubbing of stone required for de-husking seeds. In Chapter 2.4 we have seen that querns (grinding stones) and mullers have been found at Sarai Nahar Rai and Mahadaha dating back around 8000 BC, apparently used to grind wild grains. (In West Asia, mortar and pestle have been found dated to before 9000 BC.) Since in both querns and mullers the stone surfaces would be smoothed by friction at points of contact, this in time could suggest to the tool-makers the possibility of grinding smooth the entire surfaces of stone tools.

Childe argued that once Neolithic tools began to be made, they would in turn make it easier to cultivate the soil. This would come about when humans (probably women, since in the gender division of labour they did the gathering of seeds and roots, while the men mainly hunted) discovered that they might not confine themselves to collecting wild grains, but increase their food supply by themselves putting seeds in the ground. Ground stone axes would help cut trees to clear the ground much better than the earlier rough tools; and with the sharp stone tips of digging sticks (as primitive hoes), the

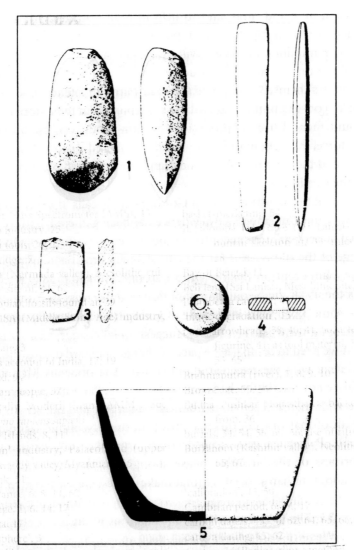

FIG. 3.1 **Neolithic tools: ground stone artefacts from Mehrgarh, Period I.** (1) Axe (2) Blade (3) Broad blade (4) Ring (5) Mortar (After J.F. Jarrige)

ground could be better softened to take in the seed. Smooth and sharp spearheads and arrowheads would also make it easier to hunt, and so reduce the distances that hunters had earlier to traverse in tracking down game.

Other developments would take place, not directly attributable to Neolithic technique, but certainly to agriculture. As cultivation became more widespread, domestication of cattle would be put on a firmer foundation. The stubble on the fallows would be available as fodder for cattle, which would supply both milk and meat, and so help to reduce dependence on hunting. With increased food supply, human population would grow and settled agricultural communities, inhabiting villages, could now arise. These communities would in time be able to produce a surplus, that is, grow more food than the producers themselves required for their bare subsistence. Use of clay and mud-brick construction would enable the surplus grain to be stored. Such surplus could then also be appropriated by non-producers, establishing their right by force, the right in time confirmed by cult and custom. Classes, private property and the state now made their appearance, based on such expropriation of the surplus.

All this constituted what Gordon Childe calls 'the Neolithic Revolution'. Since his time much new evidence has been gathered, and we can now see much better how our subcontinent too shared in the process. On the western fringe of the Indus basin, at the site of Mehrgarh (Baluchistan), one can trace the main events of this revolution, from *c.* 7000 to *c.* 3800 BC. Critics of Childe's theory of the Neolithic Revolution mainly stress the long period involved—some 3,000 years in the case of Mehrgarh—to deny the usefulness of the term, since the word 'revolution' suggests great changes in a short span of time. But we need to compare the pace of change achieved during the Neolithic Revolution with the pace witnessed earlier. The previous Mesolithic age, characterized by microliths, had a span of some 25,000 years in the major part of India, with man still remaining basically a forager and hunter. In less than one-eighth of that time all this was changed, once Neolithic techniques had appeared in Pakistan's western borderlands, around *c.* 7000 BC. It is this relative shortness of the Neolithic phase, along with the immense changes it brought about in man's social life, that makes it deserve the term 'revolution'.

3.2 The First Agricultural Communities of the Western Borderland, *c.* 7000–4000 BC

Neolithic techniques are first known to have been used by the Natufian people of Syria and Palestine, *c.* 10000 to 8,500 BC. These techniques could have been knocking at India's doors as early as 10000 BC, if one relies on a stray carbon date (latest calibration) for a stratum of Neolithic tools without pottery ('aceramic' or 'pre-ceramic') obtained from Ghar-i Asp or Aq Kupruk II in northern Afghanistan; more certain seems to be the date of *c.* 7500 BC obtained from the nearby site of Ghar-i Mar or Aq Kupruk I. Sheep and goat seem to have been already domesticated here. Neolithic techniques would seem to have diffused over Afghanistan so that they could now spill over into the Indus basin. In the Kachhi plain, just below the famous Bolan Pass within Baluchistan, but geographically just within the Indus basin, we have the

Fig. 3.2 **Isometric reconstruction of 'House E', Mehrgarh,
Period I.** (After G. Quivron, from G. Possehl)

crucial site of Mehrgarh, which witnessed practically every phase of the Neolithic Revolution.

Even in its earliest phase or Period I ('Mehrgarh I'), extending roughly from 7000 BC to 5000 BC (to judge by Carbon-14 dates), the people of this village were living in houses built of sun-dried regular-size mud-bricks. These houses were divided into small rooms, with assigned places for fire (see Fig. 3.2). There is a possibility that some structures were large store-houses.

The presence of agriculture is attested by finds of seeds: the bulk are of naked six-row barley; the other sub-species of barley like hulled six-row and two-row, and of wheat like einkorn, emmer and hard, are present in small amounts. Such cereal cultivation had probably spread from West Asia. Agriculture seems to have given an impetus to animal domestication. Goats were already domesticated and the humped ox (the characteristic Indian or *zebu* bull and cow) and sheep began to be tamed and bred from captured wild stock. Wild animals, including the buffalo, not yet domesticated, were still important sources of food; and hunting was, therefore, a significant occupation.

The site contained a variety of Neolithic tools, including querns, mortars, grinding stones, bowls (Fig. 3.1), along with chipped stone blades and other stone tools as well as bone tools. A reconsideration of stratified finds has suggested that Period I was aceramic, that is, without any pottery. There are traces of weaving to make baskets of reeds as well as to make cloth out of wool or animal hair. The people buried their dead, leaving with them their ornaments of beads of steatite (talc or soapstone) and bangles of conch-shells. These craft products and the large storage facilities for grain suggest the existence of social differentiation, in which the rich and the powerful could claim a large share of the surplus produce and, in exchange for such produce, obtain relatively expensive craft products. Agricultural production thus not only accelerated animal domestication but also laid the basis for the pursuit of crafts.

In the fifth millennium BC (5000 to 4000 BC), Mehrgarh went through its Period II. The people were probably the same as of Period I, since there are many indications of continuity, along with important changes. Houses continued to be built of mud-bricks, though the bricks were now of a variety of sizes. Structures that appear to be granaries became larger, and this accords with the evidence for further development of agriculture. Sickle blades of stone set in pieces of bitumen (Fig. 3.3) are the earliest specific tools for harvesting found in our subcontinent. Wheat and barley seeds found here belonged to varieties that required irrigation, which in that area of low rain-

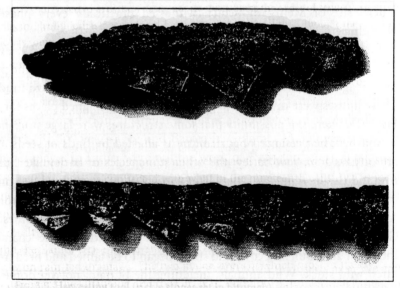

FIG. 3.3 **Harvesting tool (sickle stones set in bitumen), Mehrgarh, Period II.** (After Monique Lechevallier)

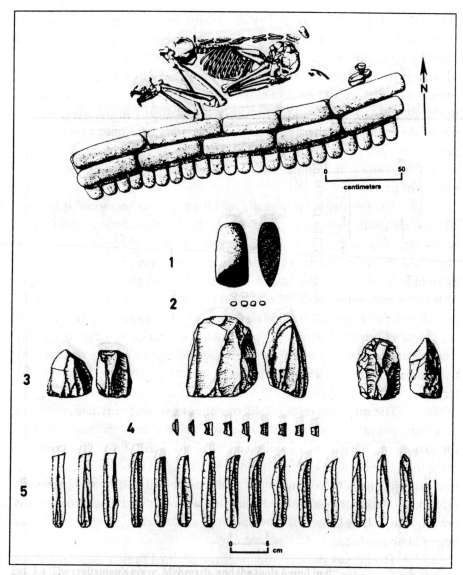

FIG. 3.4 The craftsman's grave, Mehrgarh, and the tools found in it.
The tools, arranged in rows, are, from the top downwards: (1) Ground stone axe. (2) Four turquoise beads. (3) Three flint cores to make tools from. (4) Nine geometric flint microliths. (5) Sixteen flint blades. (After J.F. Jarrige *et al.*, from G. Possehl)

fall, could only have been secured by small dams thrown over drainage streams to retain water. Such control over water probably enabled the people to domesticate cotton plants: a large number of charred cotton seeds found in Mehrgarh II constitute the earliest known occurrence (before 4000 BC) of this source of textiles, and so marks a major event in the agricultural history of the world. By about 4000 BC goats had been reduced greatly in size here, and the size of sheep too began to be reduced—these being sure signs of domestication. Some *zebu* cattle still seem to have been caught in the wild, but now, to judge from bones, the domesticated animals tended to exceed the wild as sources of meat.

The development in crafts in this phase also had some sensationally new elements. First, there came pottery. In the beginning, clay was put in lumps one upon the other to give ill-shaped but serviceable dried clay pots. Then, baskets, with asphalt or bitumen smeared on them as cement, were used as moulds for clay pots, the baskets being also fired to give the pots strength. At the very end of Period II, around 4000 BC, came the potter's wheel, a technological device imported from West Asia where it had appeared around 5000 BC. On this horizontal wheel, the pots could be rotated in order to speedily receive symmetrical shapes that were unimaginable when pottery was made by hand alone. It was thus a truly time-saving invention, which could make pottery cheap and accessible to all.

The surviving tools are still of stone and bone, as in Mehrgarh I, but they increased in variety. Of special interest is the so-called 'craftsman's grave', the man being buried with a polished ('Neolithic') axe, three flint cores (to make tools from?), nine geometric flint microliths and sixteen chipped blades, thus showing how Mesolithic tools could still be turned to new purposes (Fig. 3.4). Basket-making already implies weaving; and once cotton was grown, one may assume that, by spinning and weaving, cotton cloth had begun to be produced.

The burials show considerable use of ritual (much use of red ochre continued from Period I) and imply beliefs in after-life. The graves include not only the tools just mentioned and slaughtered animals, but also ornaments like beads of turquoise, lapis lazuli and cornelian, besides shells. The semi-precious stones are not found in the proximity of Mehrgarh and must have been brought from long distances by way of trade. The presence of such ornaments in some graves and their absence in others reflect a further increase in social differentiation that the increase in production and trade brought about.

There was still little art here. Foot- or violin-shaped clay figurines, coloured with ochre, which might have had significance as charms have been found; there are also a few animal figures in clay, and a curious cylinder bead in terracotta (hard-baked clay), giving the impression of some vegetation.

Mehrgarh was a village; there must also have been other villages like it. While no village comparable to it has been excavated, the earliest pre-ceramic phase at Kili Gul Muhammad near Quetta in the Baluchistan uplands has thrown up evidence of cattle, sheep and goat domestication; this phase is now held to correspond to Mehrgarh I. Other sites too containing artefacts associated with Mehrgarh I and II are found in Baluchistan and the southern districts of the North West Frontier Province (NWFP), with two sites in southern Sindh. One can assume that this large region, arid and largely hilly, saw the first onset of agriculture and a pastoral economy in India. In the broad pattern of its material progress the region in this period clearly belonged to a large zone extending from the Mediterranean to the Indus: almost every step of material progress at Mehrgarh is either anticipated or duplicated in one part or another of the larger zone. There were many ways by which ideas and techniques could have diffused in this zone, but, perhaps, pastoral nomads were the major carriers of both products and ideas as they traded between one settled community and another. Migrations, and possibly warfare accompanying them, might also have played an important part; but archaeology cannot identify any single cult or cultural traits shared by all parts of the zone. There was certainly no single race either. A study of the teeth of the numerous Mehrgarh skeletons of Periods I and II showed that these 'first farmers' of India had affinities with the present South and South-East Asian populations rather than the West Asian peoples. A change in the genetic complexion of Mehrgarh inhabitants seems to have come only after the Neolithic Revolution had been largely completed.

3.3 Towards the Bronze Age in the Indus Basin, *c.* 4000–3200 BC

In the standard line of succession of human cultures, as seen conventionally, the Neolithic is succeeded by the Bronze age, just as the Neolithic had followed the Mesolithic age. One must, however, note a distinction. The appearance of Neolithic or ground tools is such a break from the past—by their being associated with agriculture—that it is very rare in the archaeological record for a community to pass from Mesolithic to Neolithic on its own. Mehrgarh I seems to arise without any underlying pre-Neolithic culture. The case is otherwise with the coming of bronze (copper alloyed with tin). While the extraction of the metal from copper ores by smelting was an important technological advance, neither bronze nor copper could replace stone and bone as the ordinary material for tools. This was because the metal could be obtained only in small quantities and was, therefore, rare and expensive. It was only when iron technology had sufficiently advanced in India, during the first millennium BC (after 1000 BC), that stone ceased to be the main material of human tools. There would accordingly seem to have been no great break when societies turned from Neolithic into Chalcolithic (copper-and-stone using), since bronze or copper tools appeared as mere additions to stone tools, and were usually very few in number at that.

There is also, perhaps, a second reason for such continuity. With agriculture, Neolithic communities began to produce surpluses. Newcomers, coming possibly with better (say, bronze) weapons, who were able to overcome them, would not slaughter the subdued inhabitants or drive them away, but retain them on the land so as to enjoy the surplus they produced. Thus there could still be considerable elements of cultural continuity as the subjugated population went on following many of its old ways of material and spiritual life.

Something like this might have happened when Period III at Mehrgarh arrived. The pottery of this phase, datable to c. 4300–3800 BC, lies strewn over 75 hectares. Though it is possible that all of this area was not inhabited at the same time, there was undoubtedly a very large expansion of the size of the settlement. Such expansion is also reflected in the sizes of settlements where the same pottery ('Togau' ware) appears, and which sites therefore belong to the same culture. The region of the Togau culture appears to be the same as that of Mehrgarh I and II, but Mundigak near Qandahar in Afghanistan is a notable distant addition.

If the growth of population is to be mainly attributed to the development of agriculture and crafts (for which, see below), an infusion of new population may yet be another factor. The skeletons from human burials of Mehrgarh III show close affinities to the populations of the Iranian plateau, in contrast to the South Asian orientation of the inhabitants of Mehrgarh I and II; and this strongly suggests large-scale immigration from the west.

The progress in agriculture is shown by a larger list of cultivated crops, including four varieties of wheat, two-rowed barley and oats. But it is in crafts that the advance is most marked. While pieces of natural copper and even copper slag appear in Mehrgarh I and II, copper-smelting in Period III is established by copper residues in as many as fourteen crucibles. Greater sophistication in tools, still practically entirely of stone, is shown by the cylindrical micro-drills of green phtanite (a hard compact rock), which could have been rotated by a bow-string. There is evidence of much work in lapis lazuli, cornelian, garnet, turquoise, shell and bitumen; 'wastes' testify to the work being done locally. Beads were made out of steatite paste, obtained by subjecting the stone to much heat. Grinding stones and a polished stone axe remind

FIG. 3.5 **Pottery of the Togau Phase.** (a) From Kili Gul Muhammad, Period III (black on red slip), and (b) from Mehrgarh, Period III. (After W.A. Fairservice and A. Samzum, from G. Possehl)

us of the continuing Neolithic base of the tool technology; but there is a marked shift away from microliths, markers of the earlier Mesolithic cultures.

A major advance was in pottery. Turned on the wheel and fired in large kilns (reaching temperatures of above 1000°C), pottery was now a major

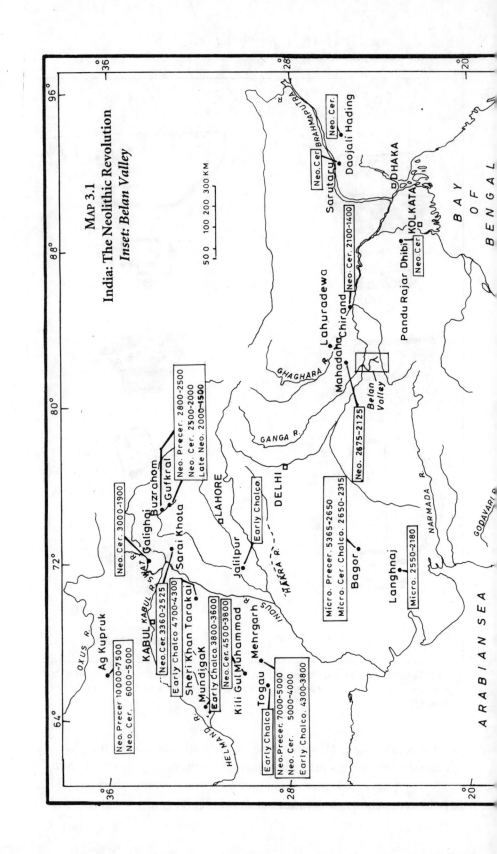

MAP 3.1
India: The Neolithic Revolution
Inset: Belan Valley

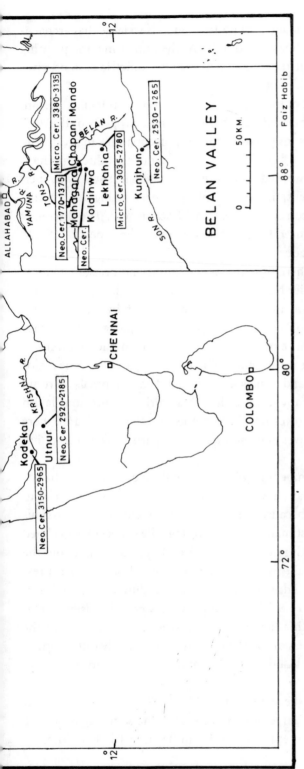

Note: Budekal, an important neolithic site, is a few kilometers north of Kodekal.

ABBREVIATIONS
Micro.   Microlithic
Neo.   Neolithic
Chalco. Chalcolithic
Precer. Preceramic
Cer.   Ceramic

Figures are those of years BC.

means of storage for all: the quantity of pottery found is so large that archaeologists tend to speak of it as 'mass-produced'. At the same time, the painting on the pots, depicting human and animal figures and geometric designs, gives us a sense of the current 'folk' art (Fig. 3.5).

The development of the crafts, with 'workshops' and 'kilns' seen in the debris of Mehrgarh III, marked a further stage in the progress of the division of labour in society. Persons pursuing full-time occupations in producing goods of one sort could have subsisted only by selling their products, perhaps by barter. When craftsmen worked with so many materials, such as copper, semi-precious stones and shells, that could only have been brought from outside, there must have been considerable external trade as well. The discovery of copper seals attests to the need felt by persons to mark their merchandise, a sure sign of the growth of trade.

There was much here in material conditions and house structures that continued from the earlier Neolithic stage. This continuity seems to have extended partly due to custom and ritual. Ornaments worn by buried individuals were similar to those of the earlier phases, but, to judge from burials, mature women now wore more ornaments than adult men and children—a clear shift in custom from the earlier times. There were apparently some major changes in religious beliefs and rituals as well. Goods and animals were no longer buried to accompany the dead to the other world; the previous lavish application of red ochre in graves was discontinued; on the other hand, there were now some collective graves and re-burials (with parts of skeletons only), a practice not found earlier.

The study of a number of skeletons from the Neolithic and Chalcolithic phases at Mehrgarh has shown that sedentary life proved harmful to people's health, presumably because of insanitary settlements and the noxious airs of the workshops. It is estimated that the average life expectancy declined from 31 years to 24, the death rate rose from 33 to 42 per thousand, and the child (under five years) mortality rate from 360 to 452 per thousand. The pressure on women to produce children increased correspondingly: the female fertility rate climbed from 4.5 to 5.8. These estimates show how the visible material progress after the Neolithic Revolution took place at the expense of the physical well-being of the mass of the population. It irresistably calls to mind what happened to workers' health on the coming of the factory system in modern times.

Around 3800 BC, the settlement at Mehrgarh began decaying; but archaeologists have located a large number of sites in the same region with a new kind of pottery, named after the site of Kechi Beg near Kili Gul Muham-

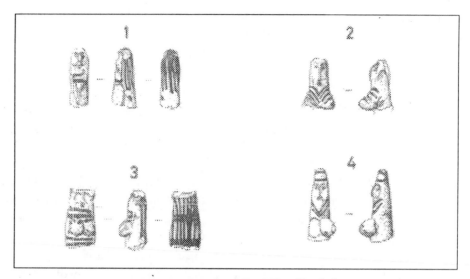

FIG. 3.6 **Anthropomorphic clay figurines from Sheri Khan Tarakai.**
(After Farid Khan *et al.,* from G. Possehl)

mad. It replaces the Togau pottery and serves as a marker of this late Neolithic phase, lasting till *c.* 3200 BC. Sheri Khan Tarakai in NWFP has yielded a rich stock of artefacts, especially in terracotta, together with bone and stone (no metal). Human figures in terracotta are highly stylized, and one type emphasizes the female organ. This may represent a deity of fertility ('Mother Goddess'?), a deity to which early agricultural communities appear to turn frequently (Fig. 3.6). Bangles were also made of terracotta, as well as of shell and bone.

In about the same period (3800–3200 BC), a Neolithic culture named after pottery called 'Hakra ware' of this western tradition, established itself across the Indus. There is a concentration of its sites in parts of the district of Bahawalpur with many sites in the deltaic fan of the now-dry Hakra river, which must then have brought water up to this point at least in the rainy season (Note 3.1). The Hakra ware, however, has its major excavated site at Jalilpur on the old bed of the Ravi river in west Punjab. Animal bones at Jalilpur show that domestic cattle were the main source of meat (over 90 per cent), and so the population depended little on hunting. The settlements on the Hakra, on the other hand, were possibly temporary camps of a semi-nomadic people, depending on pastoralism and only secondarily on shifting cultivation. This probably suited the kind of desert and scrub environment in which they lived.

61

3.4 Rice Cultivation and Neolithic Cultures of Central and Eastern India, till c. 2000 BC

Societies develop unevenly, and the truth of this statement is borne upon us when we consider the fact that Neolithic techniques and agricultural production did not begin in any part of India outside the Indus basin until nearly 4,000 years after they are first traced at Mehrgarh around 7000 BC.

Just across the Thar desert, at Langhnaj in central Gujarat, microlithic industry (no Neolithic tools) is carbon dated to 2550–2185 BC. Further to the north is the site of Bagor, facing the Thar from the heights of the Aravallis in Mewar: the dates of its two identified phases run from 5365 to 2315 BC, yet the industry is entirely microlithic. Copper and pottery intrude at Bagor only after 2650 BC in Phase II. The animals domesticated in Phase I included sheep, goats, *zebu* oxen and pigs, with sheep and goats predominating. No grains were found, despite the presence of querns. Thus it is not certain if the inhabitants yet knew how to cultivate foodgrains; they would seem more to have been a community of shepherds. The Mesolithic belt of Langhnaj and Bagor thus seems to be a survival of Mesolithic cultures like the one we have described in Chapter 2.5, with Adamgarh as the main site in the Narmada valley, c. 6000 BC.

But further east, without any apparent links to the Neolithic cultures of the west, there seems to have taken place a separate and independent diffusion of Neolithic techniques. Earlier it was believed that the nucleus of this Neolithic impulse lay in central India itself: grains of domesticated rice were found by G.R. Sharma and his colleagues at Koldihwa in the valley of the small Vindhyan river of Belan, south of Allahabad, and carbon tests of material assigned to the same strata as the rice, yielded dates ranging from 6719 to 5010 BC: a misreading of the strata was, however, strongly suspected. The husk of grain of domesticated rice obtained from Lahuradewa, near Gorakhpur (eastern Uttar Pradesh) has been carbon-dated (AMS) to c. 6409 BC; but something more than this stray date would be needed to accept so early an age for rice domestication in the Ganga basin. To go by the other evidence we have, the cultural sequence in the region appears to have been as follows.

First of all, in the same small valley of the Belan river, at Chopani Mando, there was a Late Mesolithic or 'proto-Neolithic' phase, which is carbon dated 3385–3135 BC. The people lived in huts, whose floors have yielded large numbers of microliths. They were hunters and gatherers; and so the males were nearly as robust and tall as those of Sarai Nahar Rai and Mahadaha five thousand years earlier, though the women were already becoming smaller (mean adult height: 162 cm) and gracile. This is what the skeletons found at Lekhahia in the Mirzapur district of Uttar Pradesh, c. 3035–2780 BC,

FIG. 3.7 Impression of rice-husk on clay, Chopani Mando, Phase 3.
(Photograph: G.R. Sharma)

FIG. 3.8 Cord-impressed pottery from Mahagara.
(Photograph: G.R. Sharma)

tell us. Life was still short: out of nineteen skeletons whose age at death could be roughly determined, eleven died before reaching the age of 25. To return to Chopani Mando, we find here some ground-stone tools like hammer stones, querns and mullers; but there is no trace yet of domestication of plants and animals, though wild rice was gathered (see Fig. 3.7 for impression of rice-husk in burnt clay). Hand-made pottery had appeared, sometimes bearing cord-impressed decorations. This pottery links this culture to the 'Vindhyan Neolithic' represented by the sites of Kunjhun river, Koldihwa and Mahagara, the last situated in close proximity to Chopani Mando. The Vindhyan Neolithic must have succeeded the Mesolithic culture of Chopani Mando some time around 3000 BC; its carbon dates from Kunjhun river range from 3530–1265 BC, while at Mahagara the dates are confined to the second millennium BC or 1770–1375 BC. The Vindhyan Neolithic is certainly important because, as has been mentioned, it has yielded very good evidence of the cultivation of rice, which is now India's major food crop. The otherwise primitive nature of this culture is evidenced by its cord-impressed pottery, which was still hand-made (Fig. 3.8).

It is possible that here we have clues to possible relationship with a large eastern Neolithic zone, paralleling the one on the west. The eastern trail could lead us to China where, by about 8000 BC, rice had been definitely domesticated in the Yangzi basin; and the subsequent Hemudu culture of south China, of c. 5000 BC, where it is abundantly found, had cord-impressed pottery as well. Much after 5000 BC, the Hoabinhian culture of Vietnam and Thailand had in its very late levels, both rice and cord-impressed ware. Possible Indian connections with east and south-east Asia are underlined by the Neolithic sites in Assam. At Daojali Hading (North Kachar Hills) and Sarutaru (Kamrup district), tools usable for pounding or grinding grain are accompanied by hand-made cord-impressed pottery. Unfortunately, no dating has been possible. In West Bengal, Pandu Rajar Dhibi (Burdwan district) has two Neolithic phases, Periods I and II. Period I, probably pre-2000 BC, has remains of cultivated rice and cord-impressed ware. Period II, which belongs to a fresh settlement, has rice and wheel-turned pottery. This latter kind of pottery, we may suppose, could be the result of an infusion of technique from the Indus basin, where it was found 2,000 years earlier. It would seem, then, that the Vindhyan Neolithic, with its cord-impressed pottery, was the terminal point of a diffusion of rice cultivation from an eastern source, of which the Assam sites and Pandu Rajar Dhibi, Period I, may mark two significant stages.

The rather advanced Neolithic culture of Pandu Rajar Dhibi, Period II, may be compared with the culture at Chirand in Saran district of Bihar. Here, in Period I, which may be placed within 2100–1400 BC, we have a great

variety of Neolithic tools, with charred grains telling us that the people cultivated not only rice but also wheat, barley and lentils (*mung, masur,* etc.). They
lived in huts of wild reeds, but their relative 'prosperity' is shown by the presence of semi-precious stones (chalcedony, agate, etc.) as material for both
microliths and beads. The pottery is mainly hand-made but with lustrous bur-
nishing and painting; and some wheel-turned ware also occurs.

The evidence of domestication of plants, especially rice, should not
lead us to suppose that the Neolithic Revolution in the Ganga basin immediately created any large expanse of cultivation. The basin must have been
heavily forested (Chapter 1.4), and the cultivated areas must have been small
clearances around each settlement. In these clearances—each secured by setting the vegetation on fire in the dry season—cultivation was carried on for
some years, but thereafter the ground was abandoned and cultivation shifted
to fresh clearances. This is now known as the '*jhum*' or 'slash-and-burn' system, which is practised by many forest tribal communities. Hunting and fish-
ing must have heavily supplemented plant food. Thus even at Chirand the
bones of wild animals like the elephant, rhinoceros, stag and deer are found
together with the ox and buffalo (the latter could be wild too). Even the
domesticated cattle, as well as sheep, goats and pigs, must have been kept partly for their meat, since neither the plough nor the cart was known. There was,
therefore, much time to go before the great potential of rice domestication
could be realized and full-fledged agricultural communities could spread
themselves extensively over the Ganga plains.

3.5 The Northern and Early Southern Neolithic Cultures

Two other major Neolithic cultures remain to be described: the
first in the north, centred around Kashmir; and the other in the south, found
mainly in Karnataka. Both began around 3000 BC, that is, around the time of
the beginnings of the Vindhyan Neolithic. So far as we can judge, the synchronization is accidental and there was no known interaction between the
three cultures.

Of the Northern Neolithic the two major sites are Burzahom and
Gufkral in the Kashmir valley. Enough carbon dates are available for us to be
reasonably sure that there was an early Neolithic phase without pottery at
Burzahom, from 2800 to 2500 BC. This was followed by the main Neolithic
phase, 2500–2000 BC, in which hand-made, mat- and cord-impressed, as well
as painted pottery appears. The people lived in pits on *karewas*, or natural alluvial platforms overlooking streams. They used ground-stone tools and a variety of bone tools. They initially obtained most of their meat by hunting; but
cattle, sheep, goat, buffalo, pig and dog were domesticated, so that herding-

FIG. 3.9 **Use of spear and arrow in stag hunt, Burzahom, Period IB.** Note the two suns and the (wild?) dog. (After B.M. Pande, from G. Possehl)

probably gradually replaced hunting. They also engaged in cultivation, as shown by the recovery of a harvesting knife. Wheat, barley, lintel, and field pea were grown; and in the late Neolithic phase, 2000–1500 BC, rice has been found.

There was a considerable amount of ritual. Bodies after death seem to have been exposed, and, after only the bones were left, these were gathered and buried, often with application of red ochre. Dog sacrifices are attested by dog burials. There is a complex pattern of intertwining lines found on stone, which might have ritualistic significance. A similar significance might be attached to a scene scrawled on a stone slab: this shows a stag being killed by a man, who has a bow and arrow, while a woman wields a spear, and there are two suns and a dog to be seen (Fig. 3.9).

A man buried with rich offerings, including deer antlers, a soapstone object and a disk bead, had his skull pierced by seven holes. This remarkable practice is known as trepanning (or trephining), and is attested to in other Neolithic cultures in Asia and Europe as well. Trepanning was man's first serious known attempt at surgery, though it was based either on a false theory of easing internal pressures on the brain or else on a superstition that by so doing an evil spirit troubling the person would be expelled. It is astonishing that people subjected to this operation by stone tools should still have survived.

The Northern Neolithic probably extended to Sarai Khola, near Islamabad, the capital of Pakistan, which has its Neolithic phase carbon dated to within 3360–2525 BC. There are possibly other sites along the Himalayan foothills in the Punjab as well. The Swat Neolithic culture (NWFP, Pakistan)

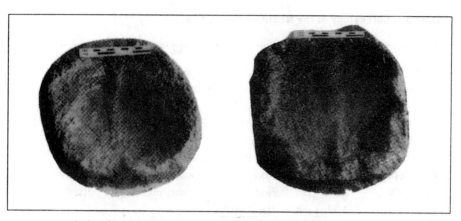

FIG. 3.10 **Cattle-hoof impressions in cattle-pan in ash-mound, Utnur.**
(Photograph: B and R. Allchin)

represented by Ghalighai (*c.* 3000–1900 BC) began with hand-made pottery, and, in its later phase, seems to have had links with Burzahom, as judged from its pottery style. Wheat and barley were grown in the Swat valley from the earliest Neolithic phase, and domesticated rice seems to have appeared there even before 2000 BC.

The Northern Neolithic, unlike the Eastern, had undoubtedly some contacts with the Indus basin cultures, the Kot Dijian as well as the Mature Indus of the third millennium BC; but it is essentially independent of either, whether in its material culture, or in art and ritual. In these aspects it has greater associations with the Neolithic cultures of Inner Asia, and affinities have been noticed with the Yangshao culture of north China (5100–2900 BC). This tells us, again, that India, no less than other countries, has continuously received influences from all external directions from the very earliest times.

So far as we can judge, the sole Neolithic culture that was probably entirely indigenous in its origins was that of the south. The zone of the Southern Neolithic coincided largely with the territory of the modern state of Karnataka and included parts of Andhra Pradesh and Tamil Nadu. Carbon dates obtained from Kodekal and Utnur suggest that its beginnings may be placed around 3000 BC. The earliest phase with which we are here concerned lasted till about 2100 BC. Ground axes and rubbing stones and querns suggest that cultivation was undertaken, and domesticated barley and horsegram grains have been found at Budihal. Cattle, sheep and goats had been domesticated, and dung-ash mounds, as at Utnur and Budihal, show that cattle were kept penned together (Fig. 3.10). Pottery was entirely hand-made, but some roundness was imparted to it by its being rotated slowly, on some kind of a crude turn-table (not the fast-moving potter's wheel).

TABLE 3.1 Chronology of the Neolithic Revolution

BC

10000–9000	Earliest Neolithic culture: Natufian of Palestine and Syria
10000–7500	Neolithic culture, north Afghanistan: pre-ceramic
8000–4000	China: beginning and extension of rice cultivation
7000–5000	Neolithic culture, Mehrgarh, Period I: pre-ceramic; barley, wheat cultivated
5365–2650	Bagor Mesolithic, Period I: pre-ceramic
5000–4000	Mehrgarh, Period II: hand-made ceramic; cotton cultivated
4300–3800	Mehrgarh, Period III: copper-smelting; 'Togau pottery'
4000	Mehrgarh: potter's wheel
3800–3200	Neolithic Kechi-Beg and Hakra-ware cultures: wheel-made pottery
3385–2780	Belan Mesolithic: hand-made ceramic
3500–1200	Vindhyan Neolithic: mainly hand-made ceramic; rice cultivated
3000–2100	South Indian Neolithic: mainly hand-made ceramic
3000–1900	Swat Neolithic: ceramic; wheat, barley cultivated
2800–2500	Northern (Kashmir) Neolithic, Phase I: pre-ceramic
2500–2000	Northern (Kashmir) Neolithic, Phase II: hand-made ceramic; wheat, barley, lentils cultivated
2500(?)–2000	Eastern Neolithic, Pandu Rajar Dhibi, Period I: hand-made ceramic; rice cultivated
2100–1400	Neolithic Chirand, Period I; hand-made ceramic; rice cultivated

Note: There is some overlap in carbon dates, not resolved. Since the order of sequence is certain, the Vindhyan Neolithic has been placed below the Belan Mesolithic, though the Vindhyan Neolithic has some earlier carbon dates.

Note 3.1
The 'Lost River' of the Desert

No one doubts that the climatic regime as we have it today, with precipitation mainly deriving from the monsoons, has prevailed since the onset of Holocene, the geological epoch beginning about 10,000 years ago. It is often suggested, however, that there have been hot and cold or dry and wet periods within it. Much of this speculation in regard to India is connected with what in the nineteenth century was identified as the problem of the 'Lost River' of the desert, but is now often formulated as the question of the Sarasvati river.

It has been observed that all rivers debouching into the plains between the Sutlej and the Yamuna rise in the Siwaliks or the lower Himalayan slopes, and essentially draw on rain-fed drainage. The two major rivers of which most of these streams are tributaries are the Chautang and the Ghaggar. Both today run dry well before they approach the Thar, the desert of western Rajasthan. The Chautang's dry channel runs westward from Haryana into Rajasthan and there meets the dry channel of the

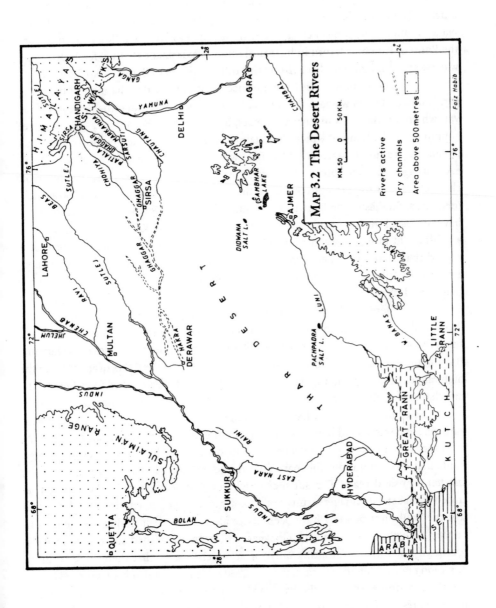

MAP 3.2 The Desert Rivers

KM 50 0 50 KM.

Rivers active
Dry channels
Area above 500 metres

Faiz Habib

Ghaggar, whose tributaries include the Sarsuti (Sarasvati). The united channel is traceable as it runs further west into the district of Bahawalpur in Pakistan, where, after a junction with another dry channel coming from the north, it acquires the name of Hakra. Near Derawar in that district, the channel throws out branches like the arms of a delta. There is no justification for visualizing any link between it and the Eastern Nara in Sind. From a head close to the Indus, the Eastern Nara flows south towards the Rann of Kutch: it served in historical times as a drainage channel for Indus floodwaters, and it might have been doing this duty earlier as well. (See Map 3.2.)

The argument has been advanced that in these dry channels of the Ghaggar, Hakra and Nara we have the traces of a continuous river identifiable as the Sarasvati which, on the basis of Rigvedic verses, is held to have been then a 'mighty river' running into the Rann of Kutch. It is claimed that this could happen because the Sutlej and the Yamuna, together or by turn, were once its tributaries. Satellite (LANDSAT) imagery has reinforced older suggestions, based on field survey, that some old channels ran off the present courses of the Sutlej and Yamuna into the Hakra catchment area. Studies of the Didwana and other salt lakes in Rajasthan by Gurdip Singh have suggested that an earlier very arid phase ended after 12000 BC, and that there was a sub-humid phase between 4420–2230 BC. During the latter phase, therefore, it is argued that there must then have been higher rainfall than today, and so with larger amounts of rain water to draw on, the Sarasvati could have flowed as a great river in that humid phase.

There are, however, a number of insuperable objections to such a claim. 'Sarasvati' (medieval and modern 'Sarsuti') is the name given since ancient times to a small rivulet which comes from the Siwalik slopes and passes by Thanesar in Haryana. It could never of itself have been a large river compared to the rivers originating in the high ranges of the Himalayas. The name 'Sarsuti' is not even applied anywhere to the dry channels of the Ghaggar and Hakra. Indeed, if the Sutlej or Yamuna ever flowed into these channels, it would have been either of these two rivers, and not the Sarasvati, whose name would have been carried by the joint river. Moreover, the Yamuna runs today in a bed so much deeper than its own earlier higher terraces on its west bank, that it could not possibly have flowed into the Ghaggar basin within at least the last ten thousand years. The Sutlej channel seemingly running into the Ghaggar, as traced from satellite imagery, runs so flagrantly across the present drainage-lines, that this too could not possibly have been active after the present drainage system, containing both the Sarsuti and the Ghaggar, had been established some time in Pleistocene, if not earlier. Admitting only for argument's sake, that there were continuously long periods of heavier rainfall until 2230 BC (a fact not firmly established by any means, as a similar study of the Pachpadra salt basin has shown), this might explain how the present dry channels up to Hakra came to be carved out; but it would not put the Sarasvati in the same class as (let alone make it bigger than) the snow-fed Himalayan rivers, because these too would then have carried proportionally larger amounts of water gathered from their own far more extensive catchment areas.

A proof that the Hakra did not carry any water beyond Derawar in Bahawalpur in Neolithic times (fourth millennium BC) is offered by the Hakra-ware sites which—much like the Indus-culture sites later—have been found concentrated upon the arms of its delta around Derawar. In other words, there was then water in the Hakra river, but only enough to reach the desert in Bahawalpur within which it ran dry.

In order to understand why water could then flow in the present dry channels of the Lost River, one need not perhaps think of great climatic changes but only of man's handiwork. The extent to which man has cleared forest and scrub has undermined the retentive power of the soil, and thereby not only reduced the constancy of river flow but also brought about a greater loss of river water through soil absorption. Moreover, as forest cover has receded precipitation has also suffered a reduction, as we have seen in Chapter 1.3. Finally, perhaps for as long as three or four thousand years *bunds* have been set up on the streams and flood channels of eastern Punjab and Haryana in order to divert water to irrigation, and this has naturally had the result of shutting off water supply to the Hakra. All of these constitute sufficient reasons to explain why the Hakra does not carry water today and has only a dry bed to carry its name.

As for the Rigvedic Sarasvati, the most persuasive solution seems to be that the Sarasvati, wherever it is described as a great river, is not any earthly river, but the celestial river, the river of the deity Sarasvati. According to another view, in such contexts, it means not the modern Thanesar stream going by the name Sarsuti, but the Indus or even the Arghandab-Helmand (Avestan Harakhvaiti = Sarasvati, the 's' of Sanskrit changing into an 'h/kh' in Avestan) in Afghanistan. The same names have often been given to different rivers: compare the Ghaggar, into which the Sarsuti flows, and the Ghaghara of the Uttar Pradesh plains, a large Himalayan river; or, again, Sind, that is the Indus, and the small rivers in Kashmir and central India also bearing that name. In the later portions of the *Rigveda*, especially in the River Hymn in Book X, the Sarasvati does seem to correspond to the modern Sarsuti, for that hymn places it between the Yamuna and the Sutudri or Sutlej. But then here there is no indication given of its large size or even sanctity, and the Sindhu or Indus is praised in practically the same high terms as the Sarasvati is in verses elsewhere.

Note 3.2
Bibliographical Note

V. Gordon Childe presented his theory of Neolithic Revolution in *Man Makes Himself*, London, 1936 (many subsequent editions), Chapter 5. It still bears reading today, for it anticipates many objections that have been advanced against the concept. See also his *What Happened in History*, Penguin, 1942, Chapter 3. A recent comprehensive volume on the Neolithic Revolution is David R. Harris (ed.), *The Origins and Spread of Agriculture and Pastoralism in Eurasia*, London, 1996, containing a large number of contributions from eminent archaeologists on different regions including India.

For a general reading for the matter covered in this chapter, Bridget and

Raymond Allchin, *The Rise of Civilization in India and Pakistan*, Indian edn, New Delhi, 1983, especially Chapter 5, is still the best text available. The same authors offer a fresh survey in their *Origins of a Civilization*, New Delhi, 1997, Chapter 5. See also Dilip K. Chakravarti, *India: An Archaeological History*, New Delhi, 1999, Chapters 4 and 6. An important work of reference for this period (and for all proto-historic phases as well) is A. Ghosh (ed.), *An Encyclopaedia of Indian Archaeology*, 2 vols, New Delhi, 1989. Vol. I deals with 'Subjects', and Vol. II is a gazetteer of archaeological sites. While using it, one must remember that it presents what was known to archaeologists in the late 1970s, and that it does not cover Pakistan and Bangladesh.

Gregory L. Possehl's *Indus Age: The Beginnings*, New Delhi, 1999, is a comprehensive work containing all the relevant information on the geographical setting, plant and animal history, West Asian connections, and the Baluchistan and Indus Neolithic cultures. We have accepted Possehl's chronology for the western Neolithic cultures, from Mehrgarh I to the Hakra-ware phase, although the Carbon-14 dates from the various sites do not suggest so straightforward a succession; but he is right to attempt a reconciliation with the sequence and synchronization suggested by cultural remains.

In *Forgotten Cities of the Indus*, edited by M. Jansen, M. Mulloy and G. Urban, Mainz, 1991, there are six excellent chapters (pp. 59–103) on Mehrgarh by J-F. Jarrige and his colleagues.

G.R. Sharma, V.D. Misra, *et al.*, *From Hunting and Food Gathering to Domestication of Plants and Animals*, ... *Excavations at Chopani Mando, Mahadaha and Mahagara*, Allahabad, 1980. This book is important for the Vindhyan Late Mesolithic and Neolithic phases. Its early dates for the Neolithic phase are, however, disputable. For the Southern Neolithic; see K. Padayya's chapter on Deccan ash-mounds in his (ed.) *Recent Studies in Indian Archaeology*, New Delhi, 2002.

A major source of reports on archaeological sites in India is the Archaeological Survey of India's *Indian Archaeology: A Review*, an annual publication, now many years in arrears. This may be supplemented by *Man and Environment*, Pune, and volumes of *Pakistan Archaeology*, Karachi, though issued rather irregularly. Especially to be commended are the successive volumes of *South Asian Archaeology* (for which see Note 2.2). For laboratory reports of carbon dates, see Possehl's *Radiocarbon Dates for South Asian Archaeology*, University of Pennsylvania, Pennsylvania, 1989 (or subsequent re-issues).

On the problem of the Sarasvati river, much has been written. Note 3.1 is largely based on Irfan Habib, 'Imagining the River Sarasvati: A Defence of Common-sense', in *Social Scientist*, Vol. XXIX, Nos 1–2, New Delhi, 2001, pp. 46–74, where detailed references will be found.

Index